QuickBooks® Pro 2010: Level 1

TRISHA HAKOLA
Chemeketa Community College

LABYRINTH
LEARNING

El Sobrante, CA

QuickBooks Pro 2010: Level 1
by Trisha Hakola

Copyright © 2010 by Labyrinth Learning

Labyrinth Learning
P.O. Box 20818
El Sobrante, California 94820
800.522.9746
On the web at www.lablearning.com

President:
Brian Favro

Acquisitions Editor:
Jason Favro

Managing Editor:
Laura A. Lionello

Production Manager:
Rad Proctor

eLearning Production Manager:
Arl Nadel

Editorial/Production Team:
Everett Cowan and Alona Harris

Indexing:
AfterWords Editorial Services

Cover Design:
Seventeenth Street Studios

Screen shots reprinted with permission from Intuit, Inc.

ITEM: 1-59136-294-6
ISBN-13: 978-1-59136-294-4

Manufactured in the United States of America.

0 9 8

QuickBooks
Pro 2010:
Level 1

Contents

LESSON 4 BANKING WITH QUICKBOOKS   108

LESSON 5 CREATING A COMPANY   144

APPENDIX A NEED TO KNOW ACCOUNTING   188

Quick Reference Table Summary

Banking Tasks

Company Tasks

Customer Transaction Tasks

General Tasks

Preface

What Is Covered: *QuickBooks® Pro 2010: Level 1* provides essential coverage of QuickBooks 2010 software. The book opens with an introduction to QuickBooks and accounting principles. Working with customer transactions comes next, and then dealing with vendor transactions. Students then work with QuickBooks' online banking features. Finally, students create their own QuickBooks files from scratch. By the end of this course, students will be well prepared for the challenges presented in *QuickBooks Pro 2010: Level 2*.

What Is Different: For more than a decade, Labyrinth has been working to perfect our *unique instructional design*. The benefit of our approach is that learning is faster and easier for students. Instructors have found that our approach works well in self-paced, instructor-led, and "blended" learning environments. The Labyrinth approach has many key features, including the following.

■ *Concise concept discussions* followed by Hands-On exercises that give students experience with those concepts right away.

■ *Figures* are always in close context with the text, so no figure numbers are necessary.

■ *Quick Reference* sections summarize key tasks with generic steps that will work without repeating exercises. These are particularly useful during open-book tests.

■ *Hands-On exercises* are carefully written and repeatedly tested to be absolutely reliable. Many exercise steps are illustrated with figures to make them easier to follow.

■ *Skill Builder exercises* provide additional practice on key skills using less detailed exercise steps as students progresses through the lessons.

Comprehensive Support: This course is also supported on the Labyrinth website with a comprehensive instructor support package that includes detailed lesson plans, PowerPoint presentations, a course syllabus, extensive test banks, and more. Our unique WebSims allow students to perform realistic exercises with the web, email, and application program tasks that be difficult to set up in a computer lab.

QuickBooks Pro 2010: Level 1 has a companion online course for this textbook that includes integrated multimedia content and is available for the Blackboard Learning System™ and Angel® Learning. The same strengths of instructional design and carefully crafted hands-on exercises that work so well in the classroom also enable students to study effectively at home or in the office with minimal need to contact an instructor for assistance.

We are grateful to the many instructors who have used Labyrinth titles and suggested improvements to us during the many years we have been writing and publishing books. *QuickBooks Pro 2010: Level 1* has benefited greatly from the reviewing and suggestions of Diann Ballard, Northeast Community College (Pender, NE); Susan Davis, Green River Community College (Auburn, WA); Sue Lobner, Nicolet Area Technical College (Rhinelander, WI); and Lynne Midyette, Everett Community College (Camano Island, WA).

How This Book Is Organized

The information in this book is presented so that you master the fundamental skills first, and then build on those skills as you work with the more comprehensive topics.

Visual Conventions

This book uses many visual and typographic cues to guide you through the lessons. This page provides examples and describes the function of each cue.

`Type this text`
Anything you should type at the keyboard is printed in this typeface.

 TIP!
Tips, Notes, and Warnings are used throughout the text to draw attention to certain topics.

Command→ Command
This convention indicated multiple selections to be made from the menu bar. For example, File→Save means to select File and then to select Save.

 QR
Quick Reference tables provide generic instructions for key tasks. Only perform these tasks if you are instructed to do so in an exercise.

 On the Web
This icon indicates the availability of a web-based simulation for an exercise or other online content. You many need to use a WebSim if your computer lab is not set up to support particular exercises.

Hands-On exercises are introduced immediately after concept discussions. They provide detailed, step-by-step tutorials so you can master the skills presented.

The Concepts Review section includes both true/false and multiple choice questions designed to gauge your understanding of concepts.

Skill Builder exercises provide additional hands-on practice with moderate assistance.

Assessment exercises test your skills by describing the correct results without providing specific instructions on how to achieve them.

Critical Thinking exercises are the most challenging. They provide generic instructions, allowing you to use your skills and creativity to achieve the results you envision.

QuickBooks Pro 2010: Level 1

Introducing QuickBooks Pro

QuickBooks has become the software of choice for many owners of small- and medium-sized businesses. No doubt, this is due to the multitude of functions and features that it offers the smaller company. In this lesson, you will explore the various editions of QuickBooks and determine what is right for you. You will also examine what goes on behind the scenes and why it is so important for you to have a basic understanding of accounting. Finally, you will be introduced to some QuickBooks basics that are vital to your success as a QuickBooks user.

LESSON OBJECTIVES

After studying this lesson, you will be able to:

■ Understand basic accounting tasks

■ Manage basic QuickBooks files

■ Work with the QuickBooks window

■ Back up a company file

■ Open a portable company file

Presenting QuickBooks Pro

QuickBooks is a software program that allows companies to:

- Keep track of customers, vendors, employees, and other important entities
- Process sales transactions and cash receipts
- Process purchase transactions and payments to vendors
- Run payroll
- Track and sell inventory
- Track assets (what you own) and liabilities (what you owe)
- Keep track of bank accounts
- And do so much more

Types of Companies That Use QuickBooks Pro

QuickBooks Pro works well for different types of companies in a variety of industries. Ideally, your company should not have more than twenty employees and two million dollars of annual revenue if you plan to use QuickBooks Pro (these are not strict rules, but guidelines). If your company is larger, you may want to consider using QuickBooks Enterprise Solutions. One type of business that QuickBooks Pro is not suited for is manufacturing, but Intuit has produced both Premier and Enterprise editions of QuickBooks especially for the manufacturing industry.

Aside from these issues, QuickBooks Pro can be customized and works well for many businesses, including not-for-profit organizations.

Editions of QuickBooks

Before you purchase your copy of QuickBooks, you should evaluate what you need Quick-Books to do for you. There are several editions of QuickBooks, all of which perform the basic tasks required for small-business bookkeeping. This book requires the use of QuickBooks Pro or higher because Jobs, Estimates, and Time Tracking are features that are not available in QuickBooks Basic.

Versions, as Compared to Editions

Now don't let yourself become confused by the difference between editions and versions of QuickBooks. Intuit creates a new version of QuickBooks each year (such as QuickBooks 2008, 2009, or 2010). Each new version provides additional features that are new for that year. This book is designed for QuickBooks 2010, but once you learn how to use the features QuickBooks offers, it will be easy to switch between versions as your needs change.

With each version, Intuit creates a multitude of editions from which a company may choose (such as QuickBooks Basic, QuickBooks Pro, and QuickBooks Premier). There is also an online edition of QuickBooks available that, for a monthly fee, allows you to access your company QuickBooks files via the Internet. Take a look at this book's website to determine which edition will work best for your company (labpub.com/learn/qb10_QC1/).

The Online Edition of QuickBooks

Many companies are now using the online edition of QuickBooks. The online version looks very similar to the traditional desktop editions but has some unique features, such as:

- The ability to access it from any computer with Internet access
- A way for users in multiple or remote locations to utilize a single file
- Automatic online backups

In addition, there is no need to worry about technological problems associated with desktop product installation and support when using QuickBooks online.

All of the users of a company file can access it through the web with a username and password, and all users work with the same up-to-date company file. It is recommended that you have a high-speed Internet connection to utilize this edition. The online edition, as with the desktop editions, allows you to set up users and determine the access level for each one.

The online interface is very similar to that of QuickBooks Pro, so once you learn the basics of the program in this book, you will be able to transfer your knowledge to the online edition. It is similar to learning to drive a Ford and then driving a Toyota—you will just need to familiarize yourself with the differences before you take off! You also have the ability to import your company data from a desktop edition of QuickBooks into your online account. You do not purchase software for the online edition but instead pay a monthly fee. Not all features are available in the online edition, though, so it is best to compare the different editions on the Intuit website in order to determine which is best suited for your company needs. You can find a link to the online edition comparison as well as current pricing on this book's website at labpub.com/learn/qb10_QC1/.

QuickBooks Add-Ins

There are many add-ins created by Intuit and additional third parties that can make your life easier when using QuickBooks. There are products out there that can assist with tasks such as order entry, customer management, credit card processing, collections, payroll, check printing, and many more! You can also find add-ins that have been developed for specific industries such as construction, retail, and farming, to name a few. If you wish to explore add-ins that may be helpful to you, check out the Intuit website or use an Internet search engine to search for third-party options.

Types of Tasks

There are many types of tasks you can perform with QuickBooks. The tasks can be broken down into two main categories: those that affect the accounting behind the scenes (activities and company setup) and those that do not (lists and reporting). The following table lists the four basic types of tasks covered in this book.

Task	Function
List (Database)	A list allows you to store information about customers, vendors, employees, and other data important to your business.
Activities	This feature affects what is happening behind the scenes. Activities can be easily entered on forms such as invoices or bills.
Company Setup	This feature takes you through the steps necessary to set up a new company in QuickBooks.
Reports	QuickBooks provides many preset reports and graphs that are easily customizable to meet your needs.

Understanding Basic Accounting

Many business owners use QuickBooks to keep their own books and attempt to just learn the software. QuickBooks is quite intuitive, but you will find yourself running into problems if you don't understand the accounting basics on which QuickBooks is based. If you want to make sure you have a more solid understanding of accounting, you may wish to consider the book, *The ABCs of Accounting*, also by Labyrinth Learning.

An Accountant's Worst Nightmare (or Greatest Dream?)

Picture yourself as an accountant who has just received a QuickBooks file from a client. The client has no idea how accounting works and, to him, debit and credit are just types of plastic cards he carries in his wallet. In his file you find duplicate accounts in the Chart of Accounts, accounts created as the wrong type, items posted to incorrect accounts, accounts payable inaccuracies, and payroll inaccuracies (to name just a few).

Now, as an accountant, you can consider this a nightmare as you will have to run numerous diagnostics to find all the mistakes (which could have been easily avoided if your client learned how to use QuickBooks properly in the first place) or a dream as the billable hours increase at a rapid rate.

This scenario is exactly the reason why you, as the client, need to learn what happens behind the scenes in QuickBooks, as well as how to use the day-to-day functions of the software. By having a better understanding of the accounting and how to do things properly in the program, you will reduce the number of hours your accountant will have to spend and thereby save yourself the accountant fees in the end!

Introducing "Behind the Scenes"

Throughout this book, you will see a special section called Behind the Scenes whenever you are learning about an activity performed within QuickBooks. This section will go over the accounting that QuickBooks performs for you when you record a transaction.

Accrual vs. Cash Basis Accounting

There are two ways that companies keep the books. The method you choose to implement depends on the nature of your business. QuickBooks makes it easy for you to produce reports utilizing either method, and your data entry will be the same regardless of which method you choose. Talk to your accountant or tax advisor to determine which method you have been using (for an existing business) or should use (for a new business).

Accrual Basis

In the accrual basis of accounting, income is recorded when the sale is made and expenses recorded when accrued. This method is often used by firms and businesses with large inventories.

Cash Basis

In the cash basis of accounting, income is recorded when cash is received and expenses recorded when cash is paid. This method is commonly used by small businesses and professionals.

Where to Find More Help

NOTE! *You can learn more about accounting fundamentals in Appendix A, Need to Know Accounting, at the back of this book. It provides some basic definitions, theories, and a webpage with online resources. More in-depth coverage of accounting concepts can be found in the Labyrinth Learning book,* The ABCs of Accounting.

In Appendix A, Need to Know Accounting, you will find information on:

- The accounting equation
- Debits and credits
- Types of accounts and normal balances

Introducing the Integrative Case Study: Skortis Landscaping

Throughout this book, you will follow the operations of a company called Skortis Landscaping. Skortis Landscaping provides landscape planning and consultation for residential and commercial customers. In the first half of this book, Justin Skortis will be operating a service-based business. In the second half, Justin will begin to stock inventory to sell to his customers, and you will examine how QuickBooks deals with inventory issues.

This book does not begin by teaching you how to set up a company but rather by teaching you how to perform the basic tasks in QuickBooks. This solid foundation will allow you to have a better understanding of the software and how it works so you can more efficiently set up a company in Lesson 5, Creating a Company.

All of the Hands-On exercises you will perform for Skortis Landscaping are set in the time frame of May through August 2010. Each exercise step that includes a date will have you set the correct date within this time frame.

The Skill Builder and Assessment exercises will offer you an opportunity to work with additional company types. Skill Builders will be based on a dental practice, and Assessments will be based on a fishing charter business.

Managing Basic QuickBooks Files

Before you can begin working with a QuickBooks file, you need to understand some basic file management operations. This section will cover how to launch the program, store files, and restore QuickBooks portable company files.

Launching the Program

There is more than one way to do everything on a computer, and launching QuickBooks is no exception. Each computer is set up a little differently and may have different options for launching the program depending on shortcuts that have been created. Ask your instructor how he wishes for you to launch QuickBooks in your computer lab. Depending on the version of Windows you are running, QuickBooks will be found in the All Programs or Programs menu accessed via the Start button. Or there may be a shortcut to QuickBooks on the Windows Desktop.

 TIP! *"There is more than one way to do everything on a computer" is not meant to confuse you. You will be introduced to various ways to perform tasks in QuickBooks—choose whichever methods work best for you and stick with them!*

Where Your QuickBooks Files Are Stored

QuickBooks keeps your information in a company file. Your company file can be stored anywhere on your computer. The QuickBooks default storage location is the QuickBooks folder for the current version you are using.

Storing Your Exercise Files

Throughout this book, you will be referred to files in your "file storage location." You can store your exercise files on various media, such as on a USB flash drive, in the My Documents folder, or to a network drive at a school or company. While some figures may display files on a USB flash drive, it is assumed that you will substitute your own location for that shown in the figures. See Storing Your Exercise Files for additional information on alternative storage media. Storing Your Exercise Files is available on the student web page for this book at labpub.com/learn/qb10_QC1/.

 NOTE! *If you have not copied the student exercise files to your local file storage location, follow the instructions in Storing Your Exercise Files located on the book website for your file storage media. The student exercise files will need to be in place before you begin the first exercise.*

Decompressing QuickBooks Files

QuickBooks doesn't save files as other programs like word processing programs do. When you enter transactions, they are saved automatically to the QuickBooks file. To save a QuickBooks file for backup purposes, you create a compressed file. Two types of compressed files are available for you to use in QuickBooks: backup files and portable company files. Portable company files are much smaller than backup files, enabling you to email or transport them more easily. The act of decompressing a backup or portable company file for use is called restoring.

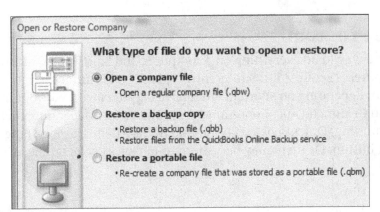

Notice the three different types of files in which you can store your QuickBooks data: company files, backup files, and portable company files. This is the window that will appear when you choose to open or restore a file from the file menu.

QUICK REFERENCE: OPENING AND RESTORING QUICKBOOKS DATA

Task	Procedure
Open a QuickBooks company file	■ Choose File→Open or Restore Company from the menu bar. ■ Choose Open a company file, and then click Next. ■ Locate the file you wish to open, and then click Open.
Restore a backup file	■ Choose File→Open or Restore Company from the menu bar. ■ Choose Restore a backup copy, and then click Next. ■ Choose where the backup copy you wish to restore is located, either locally or online, and then click Next. ■ Locate the backup copy you wish to restore, and then click Open. ■ Click Next, choose the location to which you want the restored company file to be saved, and then click Save.
Restore a portable company file	■ Choose File→Open or Restore Company from the menu bar. ■ Choose Restore a portable file, and then click Next. ■ Locate the portable file you wish to restore, and then click Open. ■ Click Next, choose the location to which you want the restored company file to be saved, and then click Save. ■ Be patient, as it does take longer for portable company files to be restored than backup copies! Click OK to acknowledge the successful restoration.

 ## Hands-On 1.1   Restore a Portable Company File

In this exercise, you will restore a QuickBooks portable company file.

Before You Begin: Navigate to the student web page for this book at labpub.com/learn/qb10_QC1 and see the Downloading the Student Exercise Files section of Storing Your Exercise Files for instructions on how to retrieve the student exercise files for this book and to copy them to your file storage location for use in this and future lessons.

NOTE! *In the following step, you may see one of two editions of QuickBooks installed on your computer: Pro or Premier. This book works with both of these versions, so choose whichever version is installed.*

1. Click the Start button, choose All Programs, choose QuickBooks, and choose QuickBooks 2010.
   A "splash screen" displays the version of QuickBooks you are launching and opens the program window.

2. Choose File from the menu bar, and then choose the Open or Restore Company command on the menu.

NOTE! *In the future, a menu bar command like this will be written as Choose File→Open or Restore Company from the menu bar. (See the Visual Conventions section in the front matter for further details on similar conventions used in this book.)*

QuickBooks displays the Open or Restore Company window.

3. Click in the circle to the left of Restore a portable file.

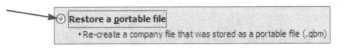

4. Click Next.

5. Follow these steps to restore your file:

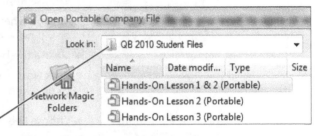

(A) Depending on where your student exercise files are stored, navigate to the My Documents folder or to your file storage location and open the QB 2010 Student Files folder. This folder contains all of the files that you downloaded from the student web page for this book.

(B) Click to select the Hands-On Lesson 1 & 2 (Portable) file.

(C) Click the Open button.

NOTE! *You can use the file restored now to complete Lesson 2 as well, or you can restore a separate portable company file for the next lesson.*

6. Click Next, and then follow these steps to determine where the resulting company file will be located:

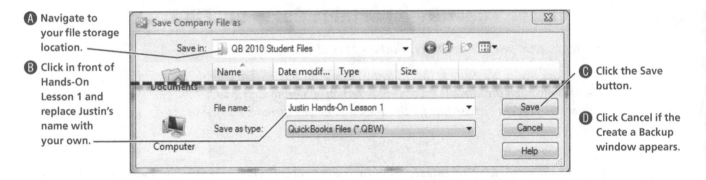

(A) Navigate to your file storage location.

(B) Click in front of Hands-On Lesson 1 and replace Justin's name with your own.

(C) Click the Save button.

(D) Click Cancel if the Create a Backup window appears.

It may take a few moments for the portable company file to open. The QuickBooks window opens with your Hands-On Lesson 1 & 2 file ready. Leave this window open for the next exercise.

7. Click OK to close the QuickBooks Information window.

8. Click No in the Set Up an External Accountant User window, if necessary.

9. Close the QuickBooks Products and Services window and click Mark as Done in the Alert window.

Working with the QuickBooks Window

There are many screen elements with which you are probably familiar if you have ever worked with a Windows-based PC. Many of the elements remain very similar regardless of the program in which you are operating; the elements in common are the title bar and quick sizing buttons. In addition, many programs utilize menu and tool/icon bars that you can see in QuickBooks.

The title bar tells you the name of the company you are working with as well as the version and edition of QuickBooks you are using.

The icon bar displays icons that allow you to access common activities, centers, and lists with a single click of the mouse.

Click a button on the menu bar to see a drop-down menu of options specific to that button.

Notice the workflow diagram on the Home page. The arrows show the "normal" order of tasks performed in QuickBooks, although you are not restricted to performing tasks in this order.

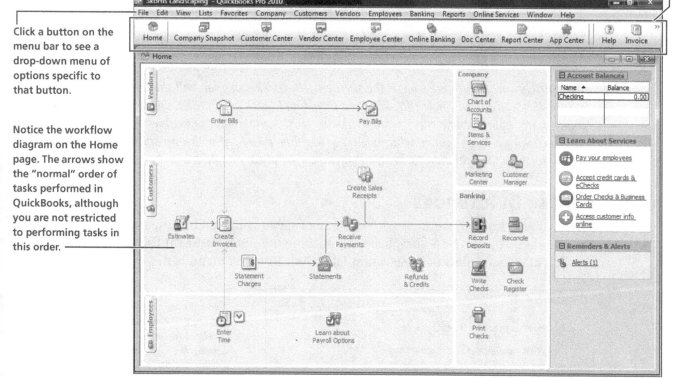

TIP! *All commands accessible on the icon bar and Home page can be found through the menu bar, but not all menu bar commands can be located on the icon bar or Home page (they would be a bit too crowded).*

Marketing Center & Customer Manager

In the 2010 version of QuickBooks, Intuit introduced two new web-based services that will help you to run your business more effectively. The Customer Manager allows you to manage all of your cutomers in one place. The Marketing Center can help you send professional-looking emails to your customers. To access these services and learn more, click the appropriate task icon on the Home page.

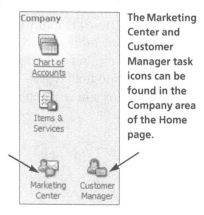

The Marketing Center and Customer Manager task icons can be found in the Company area of the Home page.

Controlling the QuickBooks Display

If you cannot see the icon bar or Open Windows list, you can turn them on through the View menu. To show or hide the icon bar, choose View→Icon Bar from the menu bar. To show or hide the Open Windows list, choose View→Open Window List from the menu bar.

 TIP! *You can switch between windows by clicking them in the Open Windows list, much the same as you switch between windows by clicking buttons on the Windows taskbar.*

A checkmark next to Icon Bar on the View menu tells you that this item is currently displayed on the screen.

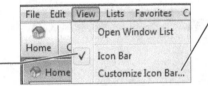

Note where you can go to customize the icon bar.

 TIP! *To single-click or double-click, that is the question...In QuickBooks you will single-click most of the time. Make it a rule to always single-click first, and then double-click only if the single-click doesn't work. Most students are "happy double-clickers," and this can get you into trouble sometimes (especially if you are double-clicking a toggle button, which would be like flipping a light switch up and down and then wondering why the light didn't stay on). Remember, you always single-click a button!*

Exiting QuickBooks

When you are finished working with QuickBooks, you will need to close the company file and the program. This can be accomplished by clicking the Close button at the top-right corner of the QuickBooks window or by selecting File→Exit from the menu bar.

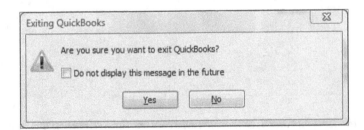

If you choose to exit QuickBooks by clicking the Close button at the top-right corner of the window, you will see a window warning you that you are exiting QuickBooks. Notice that you can choose to not have this message appear again by clicking in the checkbox.

Task Icon ToolTips

There are many task icons on the Home page. As you customize your QuickBooks file, you may see more or fewer appear, depending on how you use the program. If you are not sure what a certain task item is used for, simply "mouse over" it (place your mouse pointer over the icon and hold it still, without clicking), and a tooltip that explains what the task will accomplish for you will appear.

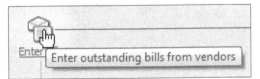

Notice that when you "mouse over" the Enter Bills task icon, a ToolTip appears to explain what task you can accomplish if you click the icon.

Live Community

When you open QuickBooks 2010, a "Have a Question?" window with the Live Community feature opens to the right of your main QuickBooks window by default. The Live Community is a place where you can collaborate with other QuickBooks users to get advice or to provide your own insights. This feature will be covered in more depth in Lesson 5, Creating a Company.

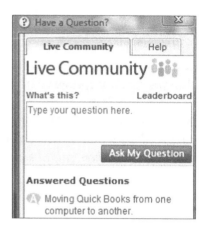

The Live Community window allows you to ask a question or to browse through some recently answered questions.

 Hands-On 1.2   Explore QuickBooks

In this exercise, you will have a chance to explore the QuickBooks window.

Explore the QuickBooks Window

1. Click the Customers button on the Home page.
   The Customer Center will open, where you can work with the customers on your list and manage various customer transactions.

2. Choose Lists→Chart of Accounts from the menu bar.
   The Chart of Accounts window opens. This is an example of a list in QuickBooks. It lists the various accounts this company utilizes.

3. Click the Company Snapshot icon on the icon bar.
   The Company Snapshot window opens. This form looks like a paper check. QuickBooks often uses a screen that looks like a paper form to simplify data entry.

4. Choose View→Open Window List from the menu bar.

Notice that all four of the windows that are open are listed.

5. Click the Chart of Accounts item on the Open Windows list, as shown at right.

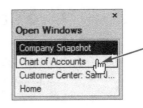

The Chart of Accounts window appears on top of the other windows and becomes the active window. Look at the windows you have opened within QuickBooks and notice that each one has its own set of quick sizing buttons. You can use these buttons to control the display of each window within the QuickBooks program window.

6. Click the Close ⊠ button for the Chart of Accounts window.
   The window will close and no longer appear on the Open Windows list.

7. Taking care not to close the QuickBooks program window, close all of the other windows within the QuickBooks program window, including the Open Windows list.

!NOTE! *The Open Windows list can be closed either by choosing View→Open Window List from the menu bar or by clicking the "X" at the top-right corner of the list. You may need to close the Open Windows List first in order to view the Close buttons for all of the windows since they may have been shifted to the right and off of the screen.*

8. Choose View→Icon Bar from the menu bar.
   QuickBooks no longer displays the icon bar.

Close and Reopen QuickBooks

9. Choose File→Exit from the menu bar.
   The QuickBooks window closes.

10. Open QuickBooks by choosing Start→All Programs→QuickBooks→QuickBooks 2010.
    Notice that QuickBooks opens the file that you were last working on and that the icon bar is not visible. The Home page will be visible, though, as it is set to open whenever QuickBooks is launched. This is a preference that can be changed, if desired.

11. Click No in the Set Up an External Accountant User window.

12. Choose View→Icon Bar from the menu bar.
    The icon bar reappears.

Mouse Around the Home Page

13. Mouse over the task icon for the following tasks and write the ToolTip in the space provided.

■ Chart of Accounts

_____

_____

■ Create Invoices

_____

_____

■ Pay Bills

_____

_____

■ Reconcile

_____

_____

Leave QuickBooks open with the Home page displayed for the next exercise.

Backing Up Your Company File

You have already learned how to restore a portable company file. Now you will learn how to create a backup file. If you have ever lost a file or had your computer "crash" on you, you can understand the importance of backing up your data!

When working in QuickBooks, you cannot save your file as you may be used to doing in programs such as Microsoft® Word. Transactions are automatically saved to your company file as you enter them, so the backup operation will back up the entire file.

How often you back up your file is up to you, but you should not let too much time go between backups. If you lose your company file and are forced to restore the backup copy, you will have to enter all of the transactions since your last backup.

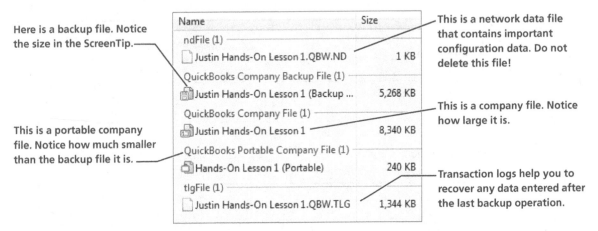

Here is a backup file. Notice the size in the ScreenTip.

This is a portable company file. Notice how much smaller than the backup file it is.

This is a network data file that contains important configuration data. Do not delete this file!

This is a company file. Notice how large it is.

Transaction logs help you to recover any data entered after the last backup operation.

When QuickBooks creates either a backup or portable company file, it compresses all data stored in the company file. This is why these files are substantially smaller than the company file. Notice how much smaller the portable company file is than the backup file. This is why portable company files are great for sending by email.

Backup Location

Do not back up your company file to your hard drive or where your main company file is stored. Choose an alternate backup location such as a network drive, USB drive, CD-RW, or the QuickBooks' online backup option. If you back up your file to a USB drive or some other removable media, make sure to store the backup copy someplace other than where the original file is physically located (for instance, do not set the backup disc on the PC where the original file is, just in case something such as a fire or water damage occurs at the physical location).

When to Save a Backup Copy

In QuickBooks 2010, you have the opportunity to choose when you wish to back up your company file. QuickBooks allows you to choose between three options:

- Immediately
- Immediately and schedule future backups
- Only schedule future backups

The future backup options make it easy to back up your company file on a regular basis without having to remember to physically issue the command. If you choose scheduled backups, make sure that your selected backup location is available to QuickBooks at the scheduled times. For instance, ensure that you have your USB flash drive available if it is your backup location.

QUICK REFERENCE: CREATING PORTABLE COMPANY FILES AND BACKUP FILES

Task	Procedure
Create a portable company file	■ Choose File→Save Copy or Backup from the menu bar. ■ Choose Portable company file, and then click Next. ■ Choose the location in which to store the portable company file, and then click Save. ■ Click OK to allow QuickBooks to close and reopen your file. ■ Click OK to acknowledge the portable company file creation.
Create a backup file	■ Choose File→Save Copy or Backup from the menu bar. ■ Choose Backup copy, and then click Next. ■ Choose whether you wish to create a local or online backup. ■ Choose when you wish to create the backup copy. ■ Choose the location in which to store the backup file, and then click Save. ■ Click OK to acknowledge the backup file creation.

 Hands-On 1.3   Back Up Your QuickBooks Data File

In this exercise, you will create a backup copy of your company file. Ask your instructor where he wants you to back up your file. A USB removable storage drive is used in this example.

1. Choose File→Save Copy or Backup from the menu bar.

2. Look at the types of files you can save, ensure that Backup copy is chosen, and click Next.

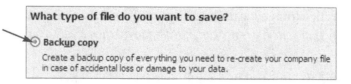

3. Click to choose Local Backup, and then click Next.

4. Click the Browse button.

5. Choose your file storage location in the Browse for Folder window. (The drive or folder name will probably be different from the one shown here.)

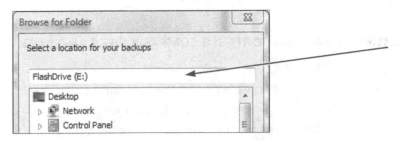

If you are not sure where to save your backup copy, ask your instructor or see Storing Your Exercise Files on the student web page for more information regarding file storage media.

6. Click the OK button twice.
   If you have chosen to save the file to the same drive on which the company file is stored, QuickBooks will display a warning window.

7. Read the information in the QuickBooks window, and then click the Use this location option, if necessary.

8. Choose Save it now, and click Next again.

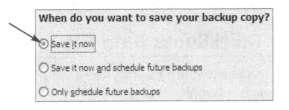

A Save Backup Copy window will appear, which should display the file storage location you chose in step 5.

9. Ensure that the correct file storage location is displayed, and then click Save.
   QuickBooks will first verify that your file is not corrupted and will then create a backup copy in the location you specified.

10. Click OK to acknowledge the information window that shows where the backup file is located.

11. Choose the option that is appropriate for your situation:
    - If you are finished working with QuickBooks, click the Close ▇**X**▇ button at the top-right corner of the QuickBooks window. Click Yes in the Exiting QuickBooks window.
    - If you plan to continue on to Lesson 2 or the end-of-lesson exercises, leave QuickBooks open and complete the Concepts Review section.

Concepts Review

True/False Questions

1. QuickBooks Pro would be a good software program for a company with one hundred employees.   TRUE   FALSE

2. Performing an activity within QuickBooks affects what happens behind the scenes in the program.   TRUE   FALSE

3. It is not important that you understand basic accounting principles to be an efficient QuickBooks user.   TRUE   FALSE

4. In the cash basis of accounting, you record the expenses when they are accrued.   TRUE   FALSE

5. A portable company file is larger in size than a backup file.   TRUE   FALSE

6. You must store your QuickBooks company file on your computer hard drive.   TRUE   FALSE

7. To use a QuickBooks backup file you must restore it first.   TRUE   FALSE

8. You must store your QuickBooks company file in the QuickBooks folder, its default storage location.   TRUE   FALSE

9. You can choose whether you want to see the icon bar in your QuickBooks window.   TRUE   FALSE

10. The Open Windows list allows you to switch between open windows in QuickBooks.   TRUE   FALSE

Multiple Choice Questions

1. In which location should you *not* back up your company file?
   a. A USB flash drive
   b. A CD-RW disc
   c. A network drive where your main company file is located
   d. An external hard drive

2. In the event of a loss of data, what type of file helps you to recover any data entered after the last backup operation?
   a. Transaction log
   b. Backup
   c. Portable company
   d. Network

3. To use QuickBooks portable company files, what must you do first?
   a. Restore the file
   b. Replace the file
   c. Reuse the file
   d. Open the file

4. Where would you look to see the name of the company with which you are working?
   a. The menu bar
   b. The title bar
   c. The icon bar
   d. None of the above

 # Skill Builders

Skill Builder 1.1   Find Your Way Around QuickBooks

In all of the Skill Builder exercises, you will be working with a company called The Tea Shoppe at the Lake. This business sells food and drinks and provides catering services. Susie Elsasser is the proprietor of the business, and you will assist her in a variety of QuickBooks tasks as you work your way through this book. In QuickBooks Pro 2010: Level 2, Susie will begin to buy and sell custom woodworking items in her shop.

In this exercise, you will take a look at Susie's QuickBooks company file. You will begin by opening a portable company file.

Restore the Skill Builder 1 Portable Company File

1. Start QuickBooks, if necessary.

2. Choose File→Open or Restore Company from the menu bar.

3. Choose to Restore a portable file and click Next.

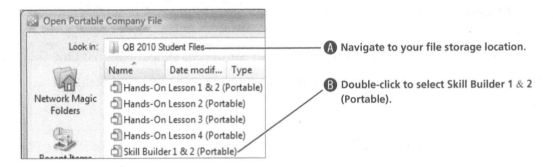

Double-clicking the filename functions the same as if you had single-clicked the filename and then clicked the Open button.

4. Click Next to move to the next screen.

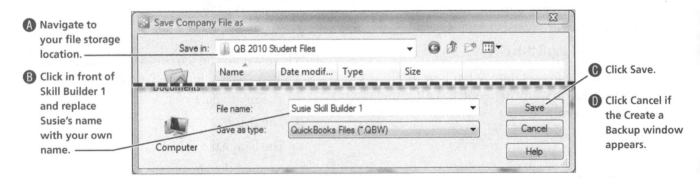

There is a long pause as QuickBooks opens the portable company file.

5. Click OK to dismiss the prompt, if necessary.
   QuickBooks opens the company file and displays the Home page.

Navigate in the Company File

6. Open the Item List by clicking the Items & Services task icon in the Company area of the Home page.
   QuickBooks displays the Item List window.

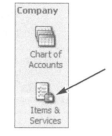

7. Open the Vendor Center by clicking the Vendor Center button on the icon bar.

8. Choose Vendors→Enter Bills from the menu bar.
   QuickBooks displays an Enter Bills window, ready for you to enter a bill from a vendor.

9. Choose View→Open Window List from the menu bar.

10. Click the Vendor Center item as shown to make it the active window.

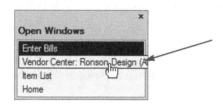

11. Choose Window→Item List from the menu bar.
    This menu bar command produces the same result as clicking an open window on the Open Windows list. QuickBooks displays the selected window.

12. Choose View→Open Window List to close the Open Window List.

13. Click the Home icon on the icon bar.
    QuickBooks displays the Home page.

14. Choose the option that is appropriate for your situation:
    - If you are finished working with QuickBooks, click the Close ▄X▄ button at the top-right corner of the QuickBooks window. Click Yes in the Exiting QuickBooks window.
    - If you plan to continue on to Lesson 2 or with additional end-of-lesson exercises, leave QuickBooks open.

Skill Builder 1.2   Master T Accounts

In this exercise, you will use your accounting knowledge. You can print the worksheet for this exercise from the book's website. You may wish to refer to Appendix A for assistance.

Before You Begin: (Optional) Open Internet Explorer, navigate to **labpub.com/learn/qb10/**, *click the Level 1 tab, click the Skill Builder 1.2 link, and then print the worksheet.*

1. Using the following T accounts, write the name of each of the accounts listed on the top of a T:
   - Bank Service Charges
   - Food Sales
   - Checking Account
   - Loan for Delivery Vehicle
   - Prepaid Insurance
   - Retained Earnings

2. Next to each account, write the type of account it is (asset, liability, equity, income, or expense).

3. Label the debit and credit side of each T.

4. Place an **NB** on the appropriate side of the T to indicate the normal balance side of each account.

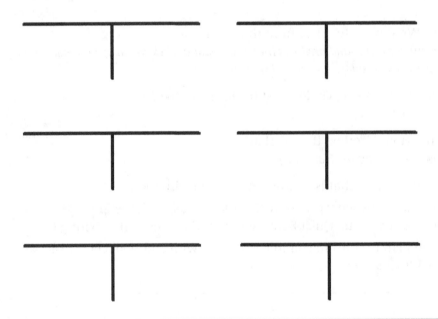

Assessments

Assessment 1.1   Restore a QuickBooks Backup File

In all of the Assessment exercises, you will be working with a company called Island Charters, run by Mary O'Malley, that provides fishing charter excursions for its customers. You will be assisting Mary with a variety of QuickBooks tasks as you work your way through this book. In QuickBooks Pro 2010: Level 2, Mary will begin to buy and sell fishing trip accessories.

In this exercise, you will have an opportunity to restore a backup file (up to this point you have been working with portable company files) and take a look at Mary's QuickBooks company file.

1. Start QuickBooks and restore the Assessment 1 & 2 backup file in the QB 2010 Student-Files folder in your file storage location. Make sure that you name the restored company file **{Your First Name} Assessment 1**.

2. Open the following windows using any of the methods introduced in this lesson:
    - Invoice Creation (Hint: Click the Create Invoices task icon on the Home page.)
    - Item List (Hint: Choose Lists→Item List from the menu bar.)
    - Customer Center (Hint: Click the Customer Center button on the icon bar.)
    - Chart of Accounts (Hint: Choose Lists→Chart of Accounts from the menu bar.)

3. Display the Customer Center above the other open windows.

4. Ask your instructor to review your screen for this exercise.

5. Choose the option that is appropriate for your situation:
    - If you are finished working with QuickBooks, click the Close ▐ X ▌ button at the top-right corner of the QuickBooks window. Click Yes in the Exiting QuickBooks window.
    - If you plan to continue on to Lesson 2, leave QuickBooks open.

Assessment 1.2   Get a Grasp on Accounting Principles

In this exercise, you will use your accounting knowledge to brainstorm the accounts that would be required for the business that you will be working with in the assessment exercises throughout this book.

Before You Begin: (Optional) Open Internet Explorer, navigate to **labpub.com/learn/qb10/**, *click the Level 1 tab, click the Assessment 1.2 link, and then print the worksheet.*

1. Think about a fishing charter business. On the worksheet, or in the following space, list the accounts that you feel would be required in the business's Chart of Accounts.

2. In the second column, list the type of account for each.

3. In the third column, state whether the normal balance for the account would be a debit or a credit.

Account Name	Account Type (Asset, Liability, Equity, Income, Expense)	Normal Balance (DR/CR)

LESSON 2

Working with Customer Transactions

Let's face it, the best part of being in business is creating and developing relationships with customers. After all, who doesn't enjoy receiving payment for a job well done? Intuit describes a customer as, "Any person, business, or group that buys or pays for the services or products that your business or organization sells or provides." When working with QuickBooks, you can consider a customer anyone who pays you money. This simple definition will help you if you have a unique business, such as a not-for-profit organization that doesn't normally use the term "customer." The job feature is an optional aspect of QuickBooks, but the feature can be extremely helpful if you have more than one project for a customer.

In this lesson you will examine QuickBooks' lists, activities, and reports that allow you to effectively deal with customers.

Integrative Case Study: Skortis Landscaping

Justin Skortis owns a landscaping company, Skortis Landscaping, which offers planning and installation services. Justin just began using QuickBooks and needs to create a customer list before he can track sales, receive payments, and make deposits. Once he has established his list of customers, he will be able to choose them from drop-down lists in invoices, sales receipt forms, payment receipts, and deposits. After recording his recent sales and deposits, Justin will look at the basic customer reports that he can create with QuickBooks.

Justin can access the Customer & Job List, and all of the transactions concerning a customer, from the Customer Center. The following figure shows the Customer Center with Sam Jones Construction selected.

You can create new customers (list entries) or enter transactions (activities) from the Customer Center toolbar. —

— In the top-right portion of the customer center, you can view the selected customer's information.

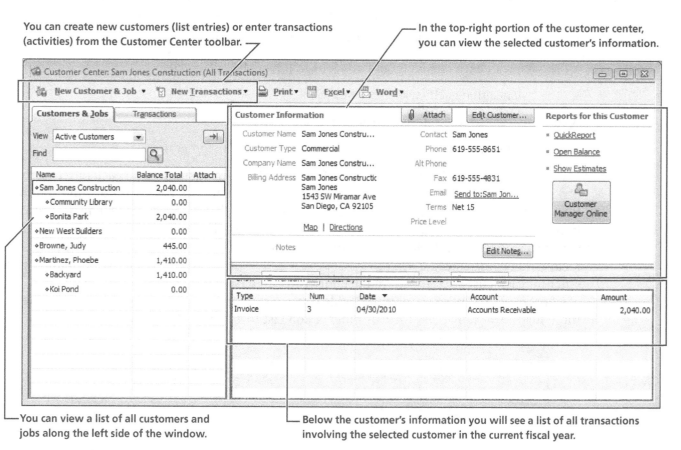

—You can view a list of all customers and jobs along the left side of the window.

— Below the customer's information you will see a list of all transactions involving the selected customer in the current fiscal year.

Working with the Customer Center

In Lesson 1, Introducing QuickBooks Pro, you were introduced to the four types of tasks you would work with in QuickBooks throughout this course. Information is stored in QuickBooks through the use of lists. Lists allow you to store information that can be easily filled into forms by using drop-down arrows or by beginning to type the entry and letting QuickBooks fill in the rest. Lists comprise the database aspect of QuickBooks; the Customer & Job List can even be exported to contact management software such as Microsoft® Outlook®.

When opened, the Customer Center gives you a quick look at all of your customers. If you recall from the introduction, a customer is anyone who pays you money. This general definition is useful because it applies to all types of organizations, even those that do not have "customers" in the traditional sense, such as not-for-profits.

The Customer Center window provides you with the following information:

- The name of each customer and any jobs that have been created

- The balance that each customer owes

- Information for the selected customer or job

- Current fiscal year transactions affecting the selected customer or job

The Customer & Job List tracks a lot of information for each customer and each job. This information is organized onto four tabs: Address Info, Additional Info, Payment Info, and Job Info. If you have jobs assigned to a customer, you will see only three tabs. You will manage the jobs in the separate job records. If you want to track information that does not already have a field, you can create Custom Fields to customize QuickBooks for your unique business. Custom Fields will be introduced in *QuickBooks Pro 2010: Level 2*. Remember, the more information you enter for each customer, the more flexibility you will have later when you learn how to customize reports. When you utilize fields you can sort, group, and filter your reports using these fields. You can access the Customer & Job List through the Customer Center.

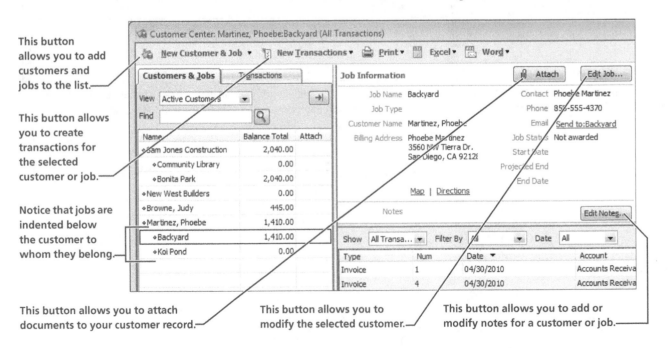

This button allows you to add customers and jobs to the list.

This button allows you to create transactions for the selected customer or job.

Notice that jobs are indented below the customer to whom they belong.

This button allows you to attach documents to your customer record.

This button allows you to modify the selected customer.

This button allows you to add or modify notes for a customer or job.

Managing the Customer & Job List

List management tasks are performed similarly for the various lists in QuickBooks. The exact procedure that you follow will depend on whether the list is integrated into a QuickBooks center (Customer & Job, Vendors, Employee) or is accessible via the List option on the menu bar.

!NOTE! *Users of Previous Versions: Beginning in QuickBooks 2006 you can no longer access the Customer:Job list (as well as the Vendor and Employee lists) from the menu bar. It is now an integrated part of the Customer Center.*

Creating a New Customer

To enter customer transactions, you must first enter your customers into the Customer & Job List. Customers can be entered at any time and can even be entered "on the fly" into the customer field on forms such as Create Invoices and Enter Sales Receipts; you will then have to select Quick Add or Setup from the pop-up window. Once you have added a customer to the list, you can create individual jobs for that customer.

Editing an Existing Customer

Once you have created a customer, you can always go back and edit that customer through the Customer Center. The one item that cannot be edited after you have created and saved a new customer is the opening balance (it must be adjusted through the customer register). When you change the information for a customer, including the customer's name, it will be reflected in both future and past transactions.

Deleting a Customer

You can delete a customer or job from the Customer & Job List **as long as you have not used that list entry in a transaction.** If you have used it in a transaction, you can make it inactive, but cannot delete it until after you close the books for a period and clean up your company's data.

Adding/Editing Multiple List Entries

A new feature in QuickBooks 2010 is one that allows the customer, vendor, and item lists to all be managed in one location. You can choose to either type the list entries or paste them from Microsoft Excel. In this lesson, you will learn how to enter one entry at a time in the Customer & Job List. In *QuickBooks Pro 2010: Level 2*, you will have a chance to add and edit multiple list entries using this new feature.

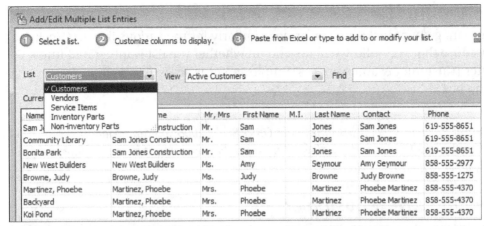

The Add/Edit Multiple List Entries window provides a way for you to quickly add and edit the following types of list entries: Customers, Vendors, Service Items, Inventory Parts, and Non-inventory Parts.

QUICK REFERENCE: MANAGING THE CUSTOMER & JOB LIST

Task	Procedure
Edit an existing customer/job	■ Open the Customer Center.
	■ Click the customer or job you want to edit.
	■ Click the Edit Customer button.
	■ Make the change(s) in the field(s).
	■ Click the OK button to accept the change(s).
Add a new customer	■ Open the Customer Center.
	■ Click the New Customer & Job at the top of the window.
	■ Select New Customer from the menu.
	■ Enter all necessary information.
	■ Click OK to accept the new customer.
Add a new job	■ With the Customer Center open, click the customer to whom you want to add a job.
	■ Click the New Customer & Job button at the top of the window.
	■ Select Add Job from the menu.
	■ Enter all necessary information.
	■ Click OK to accept the new job.
Delete a customer/job	■ Click the customer or job you want to delete.
	■ Choose Edit→Delete Customer:Job from the menu bar.
	■ Click OK to confirm the deletion.

In this exercise, you will track your customer information with the Customer & Job List.

If you are continuing along directly from the Lesson 1 Hands-On exercise, the company file you have open will allow you to skip to step 8.

Open a Portable Company File

The first steps are to open QuickBooks and to open the portable company file you will use for this lesson.

1. Start QuickBooks.

2. Choose File→Open or Restore Company from the menu bar.

3. Click in the circle to the left of Restore a portable file.

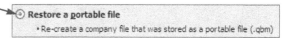

4. Click Next.

5. Follow these steps to restore your file:

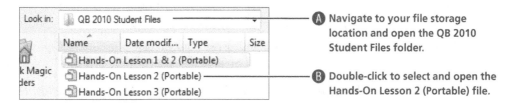

6. Click Next. Then follow these steps to determine where the resulting company file will be located:

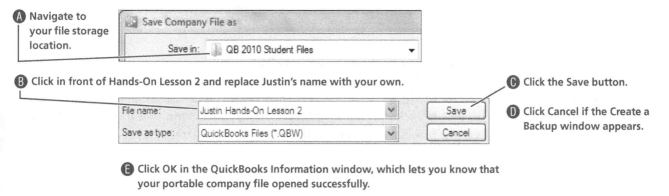

It may take a few moments for the portable company file to open. The QuickBooks window opens with your Hands-On Lesson 2 file ready. Leave this window open.

If you are unsure where your file storage location is, ask your instructor or see Storing Your Exercise Files on the student web page to review. Now both QuickBooks and the company that you will use for this lesson should be open, with the Home page displayed.

7. Click Go to QuickBooks in the QuickBooks Learning Center window and Mark as Done in the Alert window, if necessary.

Edit an Existing Customer

The first step in performing any Customer & Job list management task is to open the Customer Center.

8. Open the Customer Center by clicking the Customers button located on the Home page.

9. Follow these steps to open the customer for editing:

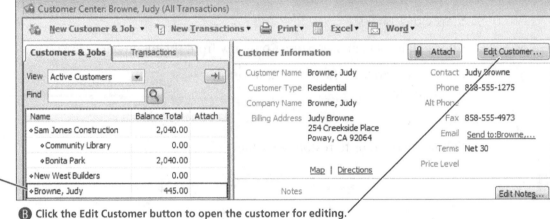

(A) Click Browne, Judy to highlight (select) it.

(B) Click the Edit Customer button to open the customer for editing.

A New Feature window will appear telling about the new Add/Edit Multiple List Entries feature.

(C) Click in this checkbox.

☑ Do not display this message in the future.

(D) Click OK.

10. Correct the phone number to read **858-555-1276**.

> ⚠️ **TIP!** *In QuickBooks you can use the same text editing techniques you use in word processing programs. Simply select the text to be replaced by clicking and dragging the mouse pointer over it, and then type the replacement. You can also use the* Delete *and* Backspace *keys on your keyboard.*

11. Click OK to accept the change.

Add a New Customer

Now you will add a new customer to the Customer & Job List.

12. Click the New Customer & Job button and choose New Customer from the menu.

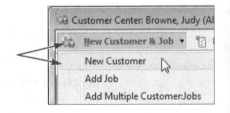

13. Follow these steps to fill in the information on the Address Info tab:

Notice the four tabs (Address Info, Additional Info, Payment Info, and Job Info) that help you organize the customer information you need to store. Notice that your insertion point is in the Customer Name field.

(A) Type **Mission Renovations**.

(B) Tap the Tab key three times and type the company name again, **Mission Renovations**.

(C) Tap the Tab key, type **Mr.**, tap Tab, type **Greg**, tap Tab twice, and type **Weston**.

(D) Tap Tab, tap Enter and type **378 N. Maine Ave.**, tap Enter again, and type **Poway, CA 92064**.

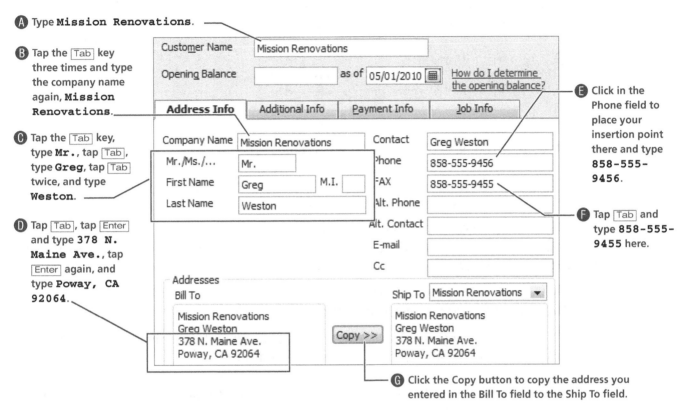

(E) Click in the Phone field to place your insertion point there and type **858-555-9456**.

(F) Tap Tab and type **858-555-9455** here.

(G) Click the Copy button to copy the address you entered in the Bill To field to the Ship To field.

The Add Ship To Address Information window will appear.

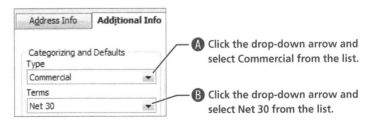

(H) Replace the current address name with **Mission Renovations**.

(I) Click OK to return to the New Customer window.

> **TIP!** *Tapping Enter in a field with multiple lines (such as the Bill To field) takes you to the next line. Tapping Enter while working in a single line field (such as Name or Phone) is equivalent to clicking the default button in the window (the button with the blue highlight around it)—in this case, the OK button.*

14. Click the Additional Info tab, and then follow these steps to add the customer information to the Additional Info tab:

> **TIP!** *Terms refers to when payment is expected from a customer.*

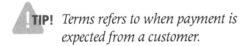

(A) Click the drop-down arrow and select Commercial from the list.

(B) Click the drop-down arrow and select Net 30 from the list.

15. Click the Payment Info tab, and then follow these steps to add the customer information:

A Type the customer's account number **2567-8455**.

B Tap [Tab] and type the credit limit of **2500**.

C Click the Preferred Payment Method drop-down arrow and choose Check from the list.

Address Info	Additional Info	**Payment Info**

Account No. 2567-8455

Credit Limit 2,500.00

Preferred Payment Method

Check ▼

16. Click OK to complete the new customer record.

Delete a Customer

17. Single-click New West Builders to select the customer.

18. Choose Edit→Delete Customer:Job from the menu bar.
QuickBooks asks you to confirm the deletion. QuickBooks wants to ensure you don't delete anything by accident; so it will always ask you to confirm deletions.

19. Click OK to confirm the deletion.
QuickBooks deletes the customer from the Customer & Job List.

20. Close the Customer Center by clicking the Close button at the top-right corner of the Customer Center window (not the Close button for the QuickBooks program).

NOTE! *If your Customer Center window is maximized, the Close button will appear immediately below the Close button for the program window.*

Understanding and Creating Service Items

Before you can create an invoice, you must first create items to be included on the invoice. In this section, you will look at the Item List and learn to create a new service item. The Item List will be studied in more depth in *QuickBooks Pro 2010: Level 2*, when you begin to work with inventory. In this lesson, you will access the Item List through the Home page.

This column shows the name of the items.

In this column you will see the underlying account that will be affected behind the scenes when the item is used.

When you create a new item, you need to provide QuickBooks with very important information. When an item is sold, it directs the sales to the proper income account based on the information you entered when you created the item.

This list displays the types of items that can be created. Inventory Part is not shown at this time because this feature is not yet turned on.

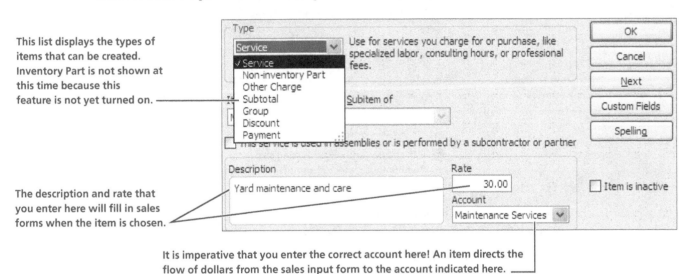

The description and rate that you enter here will fill in sales forms when the item is chosen.

It is imperative that you enter the correct account here! An item directs the flow of dollars from the sales input form to the account indicated here.

QR> QUICK REFERENCE: CREATING SERVICE ITEMS

Task	Procedure
Create a new service item	■ Open the Item List.
	■ Click the Item menu button and choose New.
	■ Choose Service as the type of item.
	■ Enter an item name and description (the description will appear on invoices).
	■ Enter the standard rate for the item (it can be changed later).
	■ Select the income account to which you want the sales directed.
	■ Click OK.

Hands-On 2.2   Create a Service Item

In this exercise, you will set up a service item that you can use on an invoice.

1. Click the Items & Services task icon in the Company area of the Home page. *The Item List will open.*

2. Click the Item menu button at the bottom-left corner of the window and choose New from the menu.

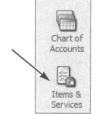

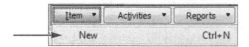

The New Item window will appear.

3. Tap ⌅Tab and the default service item type—Service—is chosen automatically.

4. Follow these steps to create a new item:

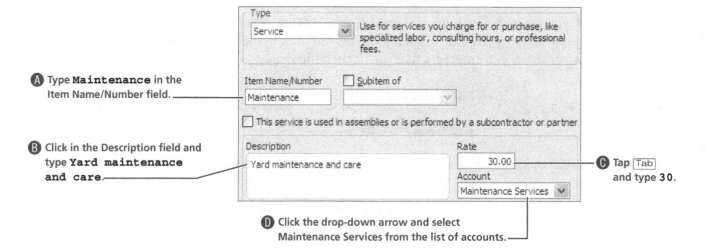

Ⓐ Type **Maintenance** in the Item Name/Number field.

Ⓑ Click in the Description field and type **Yard maintenance and care.**

Ⓒ Tap ⌅Tab and type **30**.

Ⓓ Click the drop-down arrow and select Maintenance Services from the list of accounts.

5. Click OK to accept the new item. *The new item is now available for you to use on sales forms.*

6. Close the Item List window.

Creating Invoices

Once you have set up your initial Customer & Job List, you can begin to enter sales transactions. In this section, you will learn to create invoices and use accounts receivable, which is the account debited when invoices are created. When you create an invoice, you **must** specify a customer because accounts receivable (along with the customer's individual sub-register) will be debited by the transaction.

After you select your customer from the drop-down list at the top of the form, all of the relevant information you entered for that customer will fill into the appropriate fields on the Create Invoices window. If you wish to create an invoice for a new customer not yet entered into the Customer & Job List, QuickBooks will allow you to create the new list record "on the fly."

When you click this drop-down arrow you will see a list of all customers and jobs currently on your Customer & Job List.

This drop-down arrow allows you to view the list of available templates for your invoice. You can customize existing templates or create your own if the Intuit invoice templates provided don't work well for you.

This column section of the invoice deals specifically with the items the customer purchases.

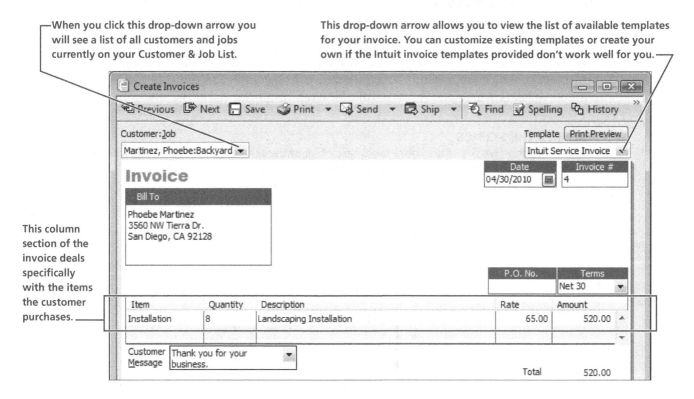

When you created your customer records, you entered a lot of information about each customer that will automatically fill into invoices when the customer is chosen. You have the option of changing that information when you create an invoice, though. If you change a customer's information in the Create Invoices window, QuickBooks will ask if you want to make the change permanent before recording the transaction.

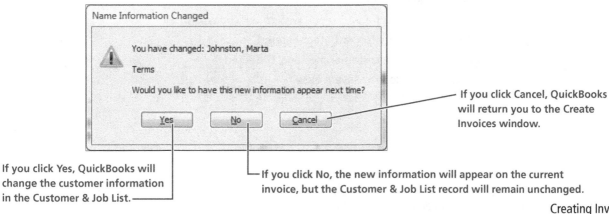

If you click Cancel, QuickBooks will return you to the Create Invoices window.

If you click Yes, QuickBooks will change the customer information in the Customer & Job List.

If you click No, the new information will appear on the current invoice, but the Customer & Job List record will remain unchanged.

Form Templates

When you first install QuickBooks, Intuit provides you with various templates such as the Intuit Service Invoice, Intuit Product Invoice, Intuit Professional Invoice, and Intuit Packing Slip. You can continue to use these invoices as they are, create custom invoices to meet your specific needs, or download templates from the QuickBooks website. In this section, you will work with one of the default invoice forms—the Intuit Service Invoice. The creation and customization of form templates will be covered in *QuickBooks Pro 2010: Level 2*.

The first time you open a form in QuickBooks 2010, the Customize Your QuickBooks Forms window will appear. This feature will also be explored in *QuickBooks Pro 2010: Level 2*.

Entering a Customer "On the Fly"

When you type a new entry into a field that draws from a list, QuickBooks gives you the opportunity to add the record to the list. When you type a new entry, you can choose to Quick Add the new record (the name will be entered into the list without accompanying information, which you can add at a later date), or to complete a full setup (a New Customer window appears where you can type all of the relevant information).

BEHIND THE SCENES

When creating invoices, QuickBooks takes care of all of the accounting for you. Following is an illustration of the accounting that goes on behind the scenes:

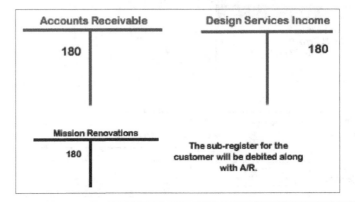

QUICK REFERENCE: CREATING INVOICES

Task	Procedure
Create an invoice	■ Open the Create Invoices window.
	■ Choose an existing or type a new customer.
	■ Choose the correct date and terms.
	■ Fill in the item(s) for which you wish to bill your customer.
	■ Type the quantity for each item entered.
	■ Choose or type a customer message, if desired.
	■ Click Save & Close or Save & New.

Hands-On 2.3   Create an Invoice

In this exercise, you will create invoices for customers.

Create an Invoice for an Existing Customer

1. Click the Create Invoices task icon on the Home page.

2. Click No Thanks in the Customize Your QuickBooks forms window, if necessary.
The Create Invoices window will open.

3. Click the drop-down arrow at the top of the invoice form and choose Mission Renovations from your Customer & Job List. Then, tap [Tab] three times to move to the date field.

Notice that the customer's address and terms fill in for you from the underlying list.

4. Type **050110** and tap [Tab] two times.

TIP! *When you type in a date you do not need to include the slash marks, QuickBooks will format the date properly for you once you move to the next field.*

Notice that QuickBooks fills in number 5 for the invoice (there are already four invoices existing for the company). You can either use the auto numbering feature or type your own invoice number.

5. Click in the Item column, just below the Item heading.
Notice that the Item List drop-down arrow appears so you can select an item from the list.

6. Follow these steps to complete the invoice:

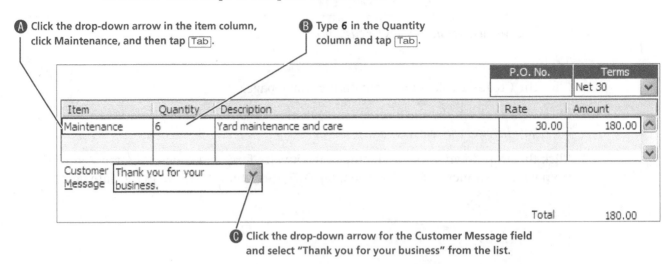

Ⓐ Click the drop-down arrow in the item column, click Maintenance, and then tap Tab.

Ⓑ Type **6** in the Quantity column and tap Tab.

		P.O. No.	Terms
			Net 30

Item	Quantity	Description	Rate	Amount
Maintenance	6	Yard maintenance and care	30.00	180.00

Customer Message: Thank you for your business.

	Total	180.00

Ⓒ Click the drop-down arrow for the Customer Message field and select "Thank you for your business" from the list.

Once you select the item, the description, rate, and amount information fill in for you from the Item List. QuickBooks automatically calculates the total amount by multiplying the quantity by the rate. If you need to adjust the rate, you can replace the rate that filled in from the Item List and QuickBooks will recalculate the amount once you move your insertion point to another field on the invoice form.

7. Click the Save & New button.
   Your invoice is recorded and the Create Invoices window stays open for the next step. When you record a transaction, QuickBooks stores it within your company file.

8. Click the Close button to close the Get More from QuickBooks window.

Create a Multiple Item Invoice for a New Customer

Another way to select an item from a list is to use the QuickBooks feature that fills in list entries after you begin to type them. You will use this method for the following invoice. If you have an invoice with multiple items for a large amount, such as the one you are about to create, you would typically have the customer already entered in the Customer & Job List. This exercise is meant to serve as an example of how to Quick Add a customer while creating an invoice.

9. Make sure your insertion point is in the Customer:Job field at the top of a new invoice.
   If you accidentally closed the invoice window, click the Invoice icon on the icon bar.

10. Type **Johnston, Marta** and tap Tab.

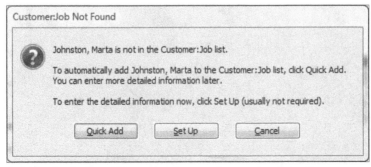

Customer:Job Not Found

Johnston, Marta is not in the Customer:Job list.

To automatically add Johnston, Marta to the Customer:Job list, click Quick Add. You can enter more detailed information later.

To enter the detailed information now, click Set Up (usually not required).

[Quick Add] [Set Up] [Cancel]

QuickBooks displays this prompt when you have entered a customer or job not in the Customer & Job List.

11. Click the Quick Add button and tap Tab twice to go to the date field.

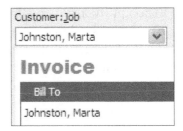

Once you click Quick Add, QuickBooks will fill the customer's name into the Bill To field.

12. Tap the + key until the date reads 5/02/2010.

!TIP! *Whenever you are in a date field in QuickBooks, you can use the + or - keys to increase or decrease the date shown one day at a time. The + and - keys can be found either on the number pad at the far right of your keyboard or to the left of the Backspace key.*

13. Follow these steps to complete the invoice:

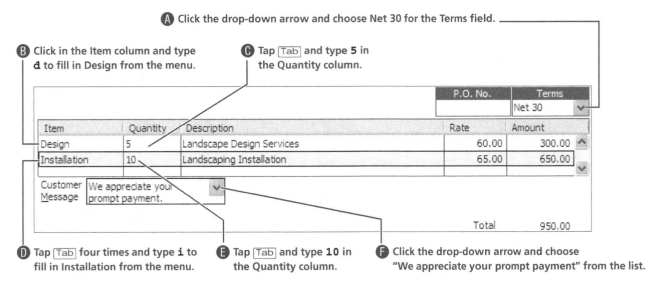

A Click the drop-down arrow and choose Net 30 for the Terms field.

B Click in the Item column and type **d** to fill in Design from the menu.

C Tap Tab and type **5** in the Quantity column.

D Tap Tab four times and type **i** to fill in Installation from the menu.

E Tap Tab and type **10** in the Quantity column.

F Click the drop-down arrow and choose "We appreciate your prompt payment" from the list.

!TIP! *As you saw in this exercise, you can use the Tab key to move to the Item column rather than click in it. QuickBooks has many keyboard shortcuts available if you prefer to keep your hands on the keyboard while working. Remember, there is more than one way to do everything within QuickBooks; choose the way that works best for you.*

14. Click the Save & Close button once you have ensured that you have entered all of the information correctly.

15. Click Yes in the Name Information Changed window.

16. Click the Close button in the Get More from QuickBooks window.
QuickBooks now records your transaction and closes the Create Invoices window.

Receiving Payments

Once you have created invoices you need to be able to accept the payments from your customers. In QuickBooks, you will use the Receive Payments window to credit Accounts Receivable and the appropriate customer sub-register. The other half of the equation (the account that will be debited) depends on how you treat the payments you receive.

The top portion of the window displays the payment information specific to the payment you are receiving.

The middle portion displays all open invoices for the chosen customer, and you can choose to which one to apply the payment.

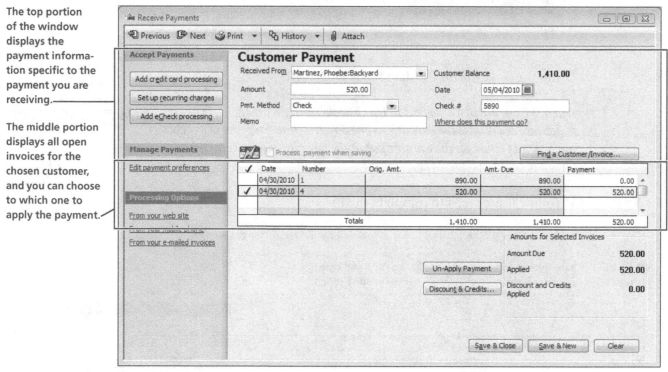

The QuickBooks 2010 Receive Payments window

WARNING! *It is very important for you to use the Receive Payments window to enter payments received from invoiced customers. If you don't, the invoices will remain open, and your income and the amounts in accounts receivable will be overstated.*

Allowing List Entries to Fill In

When your insertion point is in a field that draws from a list, you can simply begin to type the entry that you want to choose from the list. QuickBooks will search down the list and fill in the entry for you. This fill-in feature is not case-sensitive so you can type in lowercase even though the list entry will fill in with the proper capitalization (if you entered it with proper capitalization in the list).

Accept Payment Options

In QuickBooks 2010, there is a new area on the Receive Payments and Enter Sales Receipts windows that provides options to assist you with a variety of payment options. When you click one of the three buttons under Accept Payments, an Internet browser window will open to provide more information. When you click the link below Manage Payments, the Edit Preferences window will open with the Payments category displayed. You will learn more about working with the Edit Preferences window in Lesson 5, Creating a Company.

The Undeposited Funds Account

If you typically collect payments from more than one sale before making a deposit, you will want to choose to group all payments together in QuickBooks using the Undeposited Funds account. QuickBooks automatically creates this Other Current Asset account for you.

The default setting is for all payment receipts and cash sales to be placed in the Undeposited Funds account. You can change this preference in the Edit Preferences window that will be introduced in Lesson 5, Creating a Company.

Once you are ready to make a deposit to the bank, you will use the Make Deposit window, where you can select the payments in the Undeposited Funds account that you wish to deposit.

BEHIND THE SCENES
Let's look at accounting scenarios that result when you receive payments.

Accounts Receivable		Undeposited Funds	
Bal. 180		180	
	180		
New Bal. 0			

Using the Undeposited Funds Account

Accounts Receivable		Checking	
Bal. 180		180	
	180		
New Bal. 0			

Making a deposit directly to a bank account

QUICK REFERENCE: RECEIVING PAYMENTS

Task	Procedure
Receive a Payment	■ Open the Receive Payments window.
	■ Choose the customer from whom you are receiving a payment.
	■ Choose the correct date.
	■ Type the amount received.
	■ Choose the correct payment method and type any reference or check number.
	■ Apply the payment to the correct invoice(s).
	■ Choose whether to group with other undeposited funds or to deposit directly into your bank account.
	■ Click Save & Close or Save & New.

Hands-On 2.4   Receive Payments

In this exercise, you will deal with payments received from invoiced customers.

Receive a Payment

1. Click the Receive Payments task icon on the Home page. If the New Features window appears, click OK to move to the Receive Payments window.
   The Receive Payments window opens with the insertion point in the Received From field.

Receive Payments

2. Click the Close button in the Get More from QuickBooks window, if necessary.

3. Type **b**.

TIP! *Notice how QuickBooks fills in the first "B" entry on the Customer & Job List (Browne, Judy). This feature works for both customers and jobs; QuickBooks finds customers first and then the jobs.*

4. Type **a** for QuickBooks to bring up Martinez, Phoebe:Backyard and tap Tab.
   Since there are no customers' names beginning with "Ba," QuickBooks looks at the jobs and fills Backyard into the field. QuickBooks displays all open invoices available for this customer. The amount field becomes active.

5. Follow these steps to complete the payment receipt:

A Type **520** in the Amount field.

B Tap Tab and tap the + key on your keyboard until the date shows 5/04/2010.

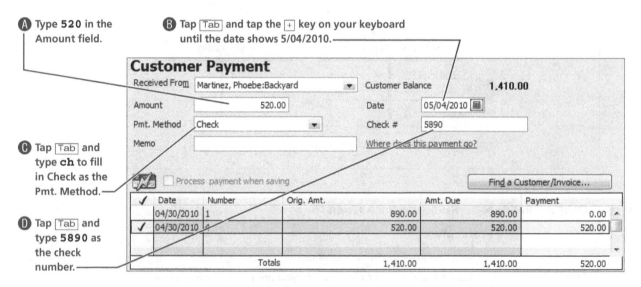

C Tap Tab and type **ch** to fill in Check as the Pmt. Method.

D Tap Tab and type **5890** as the check number.

Customer Payment

Received From	Martinez, Phoebe:Backyard	Customer Balance	1.410.00
Amount	520.00	Date	05/04/2010
Pmt. Method	Check	Check #	5890
Memo		Where does this payment go?	

Process payment when saving — Find a Customer/Invoice...

✓	Date	Number	Orig. Amt.		Amt. Due	Payment
	04/30/2010	1		890.00	890.00	0.00
✓	04/30/2010	4		520.00	520.00	520.00
		Totals		1,410.00	1,410.00	520.00

Notice that when you typed the amount, QuickBooks automatically noticed that it matched the total amount of invoice number 4 and, therefore, selected it to apply the payment to. If the amount did not match any open invoice amount, QuickBooks would apply it to the oldest invoice first.

6. Click the Save & New button once you have ensured that you have entered all information correctly.

Receive a Partial Payment and Make a Deposit

Your insertion point should now be in the Received From field at the top of a new Receive Payments window.

7. Type **mi** and tap Tab.
   QuickBooks will fill in Mission Renovations.

8. Follow these steps to complete the payment receipt:

Ⓐ Type **150** in the Amount field.

Ⓑ Tap Tab and tap the ⊞ key twice to change the date to 5/06/2010.

Ⓒ Tap Tab twice and type **187**.

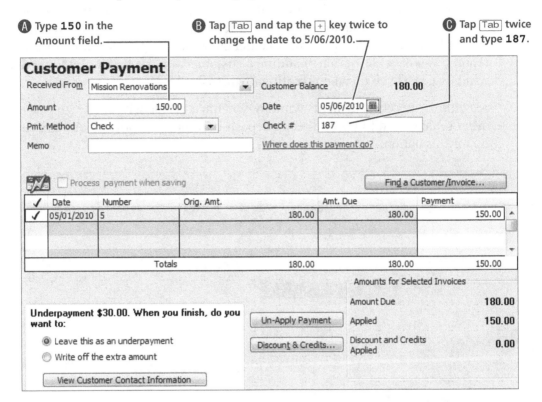

QuickBooks applies the $150 to the outstanding invoice. The next time you select Mission Renovations as the customer in the Receive Payments window, QuickBooks will show that there is a balance due of $30. Notice that QuickBooks gives you an option as to how to deal with underpayments on invoices while you're still in the Receive Payments window.

9. Click Save & Close once you have ensured that you have entered all information correctly.

Entering Sales Receipts

As discussed earlier, you can use either of two forms to enter sales transactions. You have already learned how to create invoices and about the effect that they have behind the scenes. Now you will learn how to enter cash sales where payment is received up front.

A company does not have to choose one method of recording sales transactions and stick with it. Both forms can be used for the same company, depending on the situation at hand. When entering cash sales, you do not have to enter a customer (as accounts receivable is not affected) although you may want to enter customers to produce more meaningful sales reports. You have the option of adding a customer "on the fly" in the Enter Sales Receipts window just as you do when creating invoices.

As with the Receive Payments window, you must decide whether to group your payment with other undeposited funds or directly deposit it in the bank only if you have the Preferences set up for this option.

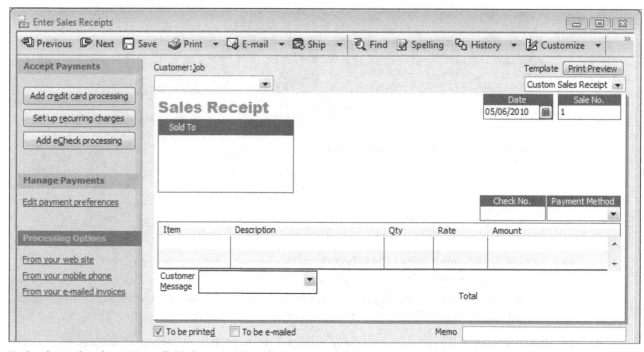

Notice that rather than a Terms field, these are places for you to record the Payment Method and Check number.

Notice how the Enter Sales Receipt form differs from the Create Invoices form, and is essentially a combination of the Create Invoices and Receive Payments windows. You can customize the Enter Sales Receipts template just as you can customize the Create Invoices template (these concepts will be covered in *QuickBooks Pro 2010: Level 2*).

BEHIND THE SCENES

The behind the scenes accounting that occurs when you enter cash sales is a hybrid of the two previous transactions (Creating Invoices and Receiving Payments), with the elimination of the middleman— accounts receivable.

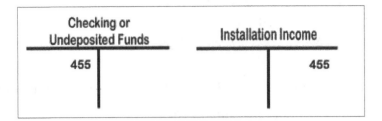

QUICK REFERENCE: ENTERING CASH SALES

Task	Procedure
Enter a cash sale	■ Open the Enter Sales Receipts window.
	■ Choose the customer (optional).
	■ Choose the correct date.
	■ Enter the Payment Method and check or reference number.
	■ Enter the items and quantity sold.
	■ Select a Customer Message (if desired).
	■ Decide whether to group with other undeposited funds or deposit it directly into your bank account.
	■ Click Save & Close or Save & New.

In this exercise, you will receive a payment at the time of the sale.

Record a Cash Sale for a Specific Customer

Create Sales
Receipts

1. Click the Create Sales Receipts task icon on the Home page.
   The Enter Sales Receipts window will open with the insertion point in the Customer:Job field.

2. Type **b** in order for QuickBooks to bring up Browne, Judy, and tap Tab three times.

3. Follow these steps to complete the cash sale:

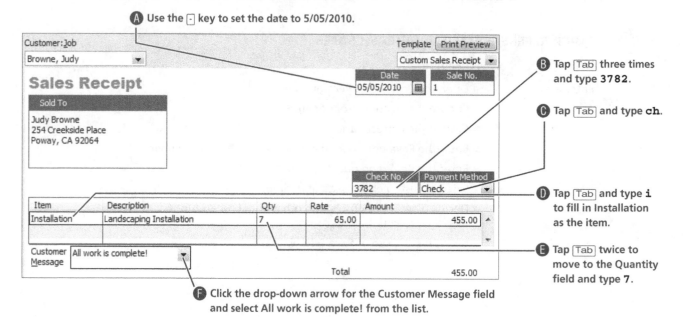

Ⓐ Use the ⦁ key to set the date to 5/05/2010.

Ⓑ Tap Tab three times and type **3782**.

Ⓒ Tap Tab and type **ch**.

Ⓓ Tap Tab and type **i** to fill in Installation as the item.

Ⓔ Tap Tab twice to move to the Quantity field and type **7**.

Ⓕ Click the drop-down arrow for the Customer Message field and select All work is complete! from the list.

4. Click the Save & New button once you have ensured that you have entered all information correctly.
   Your insertion point should be in the Customer:Job field of a new Enter Sales Receipt window. If it isn't, click the Sales Receipts task icon on the Home page.

Record a Sales Receipt Without a Specified Customer

Since accounts receivable is not affected when you enter a cash sale, you can create a sale without choosing a customer. This may come in handy if you sell something to someone just once and don't want that customer on your Customer & Job List.

5. Tap Tab three times to move to the date field.

6. Follow these steps to complete the sales receipt:

Ⓐ Use the ⊞ key to change the date to 5/08/2010.

Ⓑ Tap [Tab] four times and type **c** to fill in Cash as the payment method.

Ⓒ Tap [Tab] and type **i**; the item Installation will fill in for you.

Ⓓ Tap [Tab] twice, type a **4**, and tap [Tab] for QuickBooks to calculate the amount.

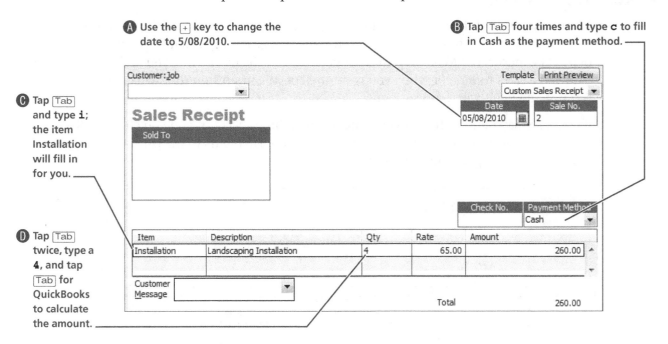

7. Click the Save & Close button; your sales receipt will be recorded and the window will close.

This transaction will debit Undeposited Funds and credit Installation Income, but there will be no customer tracked. The purpose of selecting a customer for a sales receipt is to ensure that you can produce meaningful customer reports such as Sales by Customer Summary, if they are important to your business.

Making Deposits

If you have utilized the Undeposited Funds account, you will need to take one more step to move your payments to your bank account. This step is accomplished through the Make Deposits window. The Make Deposits window can also be used when you make a sale and do not need a sales receipt, or when you want to deposit a lump sum that will credit an income account and debit your bank account.

If you have payments sitting in your Undeposited Funds account and you click the Record Deposits task icon on the Home page, you will get the Payments to Deposit window where you can choose which payments you want to deposit.

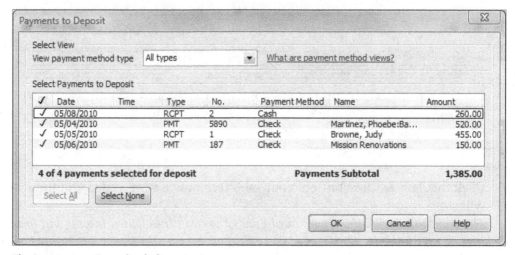

The Payments to Deposit window

You can always click OK if you are not ready to deposit the payments shown in the window yet still need to work with the Make Deposits window.

By clicking this drop-down arrow, you can select any bank account that you have set up (you only have one bank account at this time, Checking).

The Memo fields are optional, but keep in mind that you can display your memos on reports.

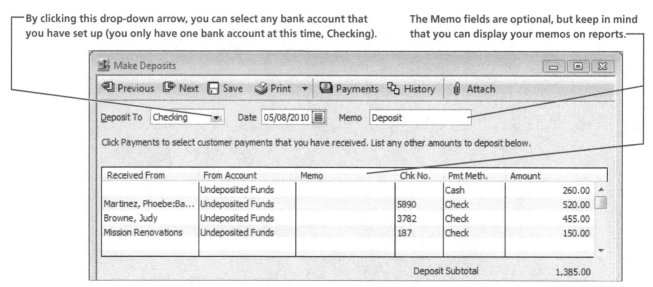

The Make Deposits window. You can click the Print button to print a detailed report of your deposits, including deposit slips if you choose to purchase and use them.

BEHIND THE SCENES

If you make deposits from your Undeposited Funds account, the following accounting will occur behind the scenes:

Undeposited Funds	Checking
895	895

If you use the Make Deposits window to record sales, the accounting involved is:

Checking	Installation Income
400	400

QUICK REFERENCE: MAKING DEPOSITS

Task	Procedure
Make a deposit from undeposited funds	■ Choose Banking→Make Deposits from the menu bar; the Payments to Deposit window will appear. ■ Choose all of the payments you want to deposit. ■ Click OK to move on to the Make Deposits window. ■ Choose the correct bank account for the deposit. ■ Enter the correct date for the deposit. ■ Click Save & Close or Save & New.
Make a deposit directly to checking	■ Choose Banking→Make Deposits from the menu bar. ■ Click OK if the Payments to Deposit window appears. ■ Choose the correct bank account for the deposit. ■ Enter the correct date for the deposit. ■ Enter all of the deposit information including the customer (if desired), account, and payment method and amount. ■ Click Save & Close or Save & New.

Hands-On 2.6   Use the Make Deposits Window

In this exercise, you will work with the Make Deposits window to deposit funds from the Undeposited Funds account and to make a deposit without a sales form.

Deposit Funds from the Undeposited Funds Account

1. Click the Record Deposits task icon on the Home page.
   The Payments to Deposit window will open since you currently have payments waiting in the Undeposited Funds account.

2. Click the Select All button and QuickBooks will place a checkmark to the left of all four payments waiting to be deposited.
   Notice that after you click the Select All button it is grayed out. It is no longer a valid selection since all payments are already selected.

3. Click OK to accept the payments for deposit and move on to the Make Deposits window.

4. Tap Tab. Then tap + to change the date to 05/08/10, if necessary.

5. Click the Save & New button to make the deposit to your checking account. Leave the Make Deposits window open for the next step.
   Your insertion point should be in the Deposit To field of a new Make Deposits window. If it is not there, choose Banking→Make Deposits from the menu bar.

Make a Deposit Without Specifying a Customer

Justin rented a booth at the local Garden Club Show and offered design advice for $25 per customer. He wants to record the entire amount as a sale without tracking individual customers.

6. Tap Tab to move to the date field.

7. Follow these steps to complete the deposit:

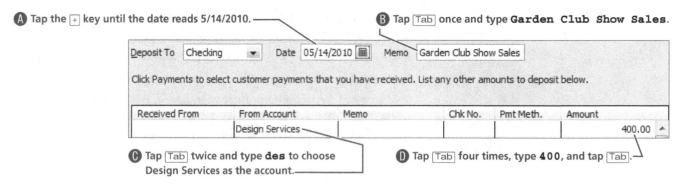

Ⓐ Tap the + key until the date reads 5/14/2010.

Ⓑ Tap Tab once and type **Garden Club Show Sales.**

Ⓒ Tap Tab twice and type **des** to choose Design Services as the account.

Ⓓ Tap Tab four times, type **400**, and tap Tab.

*You have to type the first three letters of the account name since Depreciation Expense will fill in when you type the first two letters. Note that you do not fill in the item here, but rather the appropriate income account. You **cannot** leave this field blank as you must specify the account that will be credited since you will be debiting a bank account with the deposit.*

8. Click the Save & Close button and your deposit will be recorded and the window will close.

Working with Customer-Related Reports

Once you have recorded your customer-related transactions, QuickBooks has many reports that you can produce to view your data. These preset reports can be divided into three main categories:

- List reports display entries within a names list.
- Summary reports subtotal your data and provide a summary.
- Transaction reports show each transaction that makes up the subtotal found in a summary report.

The Report Center

The Report Center has been greatly improved in the 2010 version of QuickBooks, providing users with more ways to access and display data. It is a helpful tool, as it allows you to learn about different types of reports without having to create them by trial and error. It includes sample reports and descriptions of the type of information each report provides.

The four tabs at the top of the Report Center window allow you to view the reports that come standard with QuickBooks, the reports that you have memorized, your favorite reports, and the reports that you have run recently.

Above the example of each report you will find its name and an explanation of the type of information it will provide for you.

Along the left side are the different categories of reports available.

These three buttons allow you to change how you view the information contained in the Report Center.

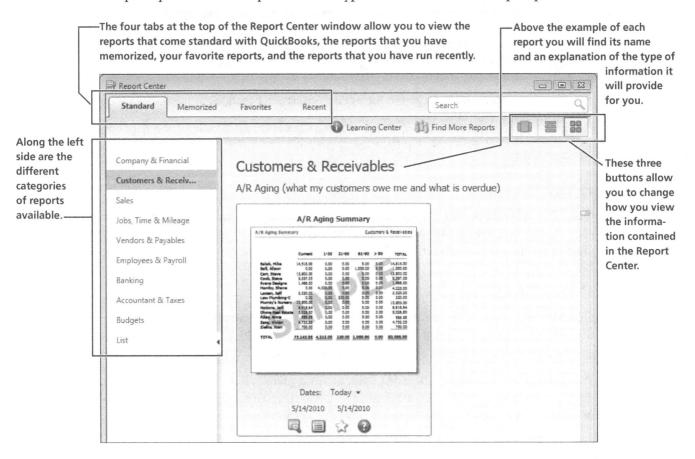

The Report Window Toolbar

The basic report toolbar is shown in the following illustration. You may also see additional buttons that are specific to certain reports.

REPORT TOOLBAR BUTTON FUNCTIONS

Button	Function
Modify Report...	This button displays a window that allows you to make many modifications to the report, including filtering, formatting, display properties and header/footer properties.
Memorize...	This button allows you to memorize the settings of the report so you can easily run it again.
Print...	This button opens the Print Report window, where you can choose to print or print preview the report.
E-mail	This button allows you to email a copy of the report. This is a feature available in QuickBooks 2004 and newer. You must register with Intuit to use this service.
Export...	You can export the report to Microsoft Excel or as a comma-separated values file.
Hide Header / Show Header	These buttons toggle back and forth. If the header is visible, the Hide Header button appears and if the header is not visible the Show Header button appears.
Refresh	This button allows you to refresh the report after changes to the data have been made.
Sort By Default	This drop-down list allows you to determine how your report data will be sorted. The options available on this list are determined by the nature of the report.

QuickReports

QuickReports can be run from the various center windows and they show all the transactions recorded in QuickBooks for a particular list record. You will use this report to get a quick snapshot of all customer transactions for Mission Renovations.

QuickZoom

QuickBooks has a great feature called QuickZoom. This feature allows you to zoom through underlying sub-reports until you reach the form where the data were originally entered. This can be extremely useful if you have questions as to where a figure in a report comes from.

When you see the zoom pointer ⌕, you are at a place where you can double-click to dive deeper into your data. The number of layers you have to zoom through before you get to your original form depends on the type of report (or graph) with which you start.

QUICK REFERENCE: WORKING WITH REPORTS

Task	Procedure
Produce a QuickReport	■ Open the center that contains the record on which you wish to run the report. ■ Click the list entry. ■ Click the QuickReport link at the right of the center window. ■ Set the correct date range.
Produce a report using the Report Center	■ Click the Report Center button on the icon bar. ■ Choose the category for the type of report you wish to produce on the left side of the window. ■ Click the report you wish to run from the right side of the window.
Use the QuickZoom feature	■ Place your mouse pointer over your report. ■ When you see the zoom pointer you are at a place where you can QuickZoom through your information. ■ Double-click with the zoom pointer to find the source of the numbers in your report.
Print or print preview a report	■ Produce the report you wish to print. ■ Click the Print button on the report toolbar. ■ Click Preview to see how the report will look printed. ■ Click Print to send a copy of the report to the indicated printer.

 Hands-On 2.7   **Produce Customer-Related Reports**

In this exercise, you will run various reports related to customer records and transactions.

Run a Customer Quick Report

1. Open the Customer Center by clicking the button on the icon bar.

2. Single-click Mission Renovations to select it.
   You must always select the list item on which you wish to run a report.

3. Click the QuickReport link at the right of the Customer Center window.
   If you cannot see the QuickReport link, either maximize the Customer Center window or use the sizing arrows to make the window wider.

4. Change the Dates to All by typing **a** to select All from the Dates list.
   Your report should display the invoice for and payment from Mission Renovations.

TIP! *When you first run a report, the Dates field is selected and typing **a** will choose All from the Dates list.*

5. Choose Window→Close All from the menu bar.

TIP! *Often you will have many windows open within QuickBooks simultaneously; the Window→Close All command allows you to close them all at once.*

View the Customer Contact List Report

Next you will use the Report Center to create a report that shows contact information for all of your customers.

6. Choose Reports→Report Center from the menu bar.
The Report Center will be displayed after a few moments.

7. Follow these steps to display the report:

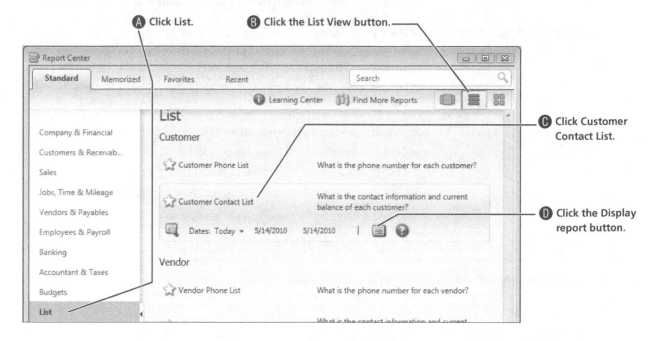

8. Close the Customer Contact List report by clicking the Close button for the window.

Create a Customer-Related Summary Report

Now you will help Justin create a report that shows him how much each customer owes, along with whether they are current on their payments. The Report Center should still be displayed. If it is not, choose Reports→Report Center from the menu bar.

9. Follow these steps to create an A/R Aging Summary report:

A Click Customers & Receivables.

B Click A/R Aging Summary.

C Click the Display report button.

D Type **a** to choose All as the date range.

10. Click the Print button on the report toolbar. *The Print Reports dialog box will appear.*

11. Click the Preview button.

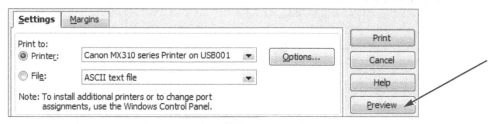

You will now see how the report would appear if you were to print it.

12. Click the [Close] Close button on the Print Preview window toolbar.

13. Click Cancel in the Print Reports window.

14. Close the A/R Aging Summary report by clicking the Close button for the window. Click No when asked if you want to memorize the report.

Create a Customer-Related Detail Report

Next you will have an opportunity to create a report that will show you an itemized report with the balance owed by each customer. The Report Center should still be displayed. If it is not, choose Reports→Report Center from the menu bar.

15. Follow these steps to create a Custom Balance Detail report:

Ⓐ Ensure Customers & Receivables is still selected.

Ⓑ Scroll down until Customer Balance Detail is displayed.

Ⓒ Click Customer Balance Detail.

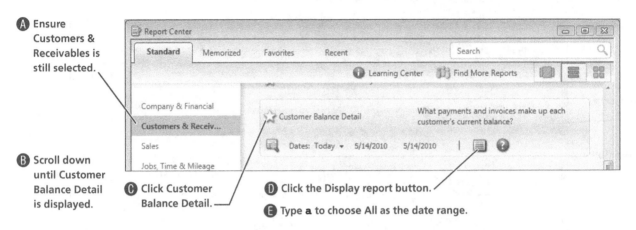

Ⓓ Click the Display report button.

Ⓔ Type **a** to choose All as the date range.

Leave the report displayed; you will use it for the next section.

Use QuickZoom in a Report

Justin wants to see the full details for invoice #5. You will use QuickZoom in order to do this for him.

16. Move your mouse pointer over the report and notice how it changes shape depending on what it is over. Place your mouse pointer over invoice 5 for Mission Renovations (look at the following example), until you see the QuickZoom pointer.

17. Double-click with the QuickZoom pointer over invoice 5 for Mission Renovations. *QuickBooks will open and display the invoice where the transaction was originally entered.*

18. Select Window→Close All from the menu bar. Click No when asked if you want to memorize the report.

19. Choose the appropriate option for your situation:

   ■ If you are continuing on to Lesson 3 or to the end-of-lesson exercises, leave QuickBooks open and complete the Concepts Review section.

   ■ If you are finished working in QuickBooks, Choose File→Exit from the menu bar.

Concepts Review

True/False Questions

1. A customer is a person or a company to whom or which you pay money.   TRUE   FALSE

2. You can delete a customer from the Customer & Job List as long as that customer hasn't been used in a transaction.   TRUE   FALSE

3. If you change the name of a customer, it will only be reflected in new transactions for the customer.   TRUE   FALSE

4. If you want to bill a customer for a service, the service must first be set up as an item.   TRUE   FALSE

5. When you use a sales receipt to bill a customer, Accounts Receivable will be debited.   TRUE   FALSE

6. When you receive a payment from a customer, you have to deposit it into the Undeposited Funds account.   TRUE   FALSE

7. When you choose to open the Make Deposits window, the Payments to Deposit window will open if there are any deposits in the Undeposited Funds account.   TRUE   FALSE

8. When you make a deposit to Checking, your checking account will be credited.   TRUE   FALSE

9. The Report Center windows tells what the selected report will tell you if you choose to create it.   TRUE   FALSE

10. You can enter customers at any time, even "on the fly."   TRUE   FALSE

Multiple Choice Questions

1. Information is stored in QuickBooks through the use of:
   a. Activities
   b. Reports
   c. Lists
   d. Transactions

2. What account is debited when invoices are created?
   a. Accounts Payable
   b. Accounts Receivable
   c. Checking
   d. Income Account

3. What type of account is the Undeposited Funds account?
   a. Asset
   b. Liability
   c. Equity
   d. Income

4. What tool can you use if you have questions as to where a figure in a report comes from?
   a. QuickReport
   b. Report Find
   c. QuickZoom
   d. Transaction Seeker

 # Skill Builders

Before you begin these exercises, restore the Skill Builder 2 portable company file from your file storage location and type your name as the first word in the filename (e.g., Susie Skill Builder 2) before saving it in your file storage location. If you need to review how to open a portable company file, look at Hands-On 2.1. You may also use the file you restored for the Lesson 1 Skill Builder exercise, if you wish.

Skill Builder 2.1   Manage Your Customer & Job List

In this exercise, you will create, edit, and delete Customer & Job List entries for Susie.

Edit a Customer Record

1. Open the Customer Center by choosing Customers→Customer Center from the menu bar.

2. Double-click Lisa Mills to open it for editing.

3. Click in the box to the left of Do not display this message in the future. Click OK in the New Feature window, if necessary.

4. Change the customer's name to **Lisa Silvers**.
   You will have to change the name in five separate locations. You can use the Copy button to copy the Bill to Address to the Ship to Address field. You will need to edit the Ship To address for Esther Busch. This customer's name will change in all of the transactions that she was involved in, as well as in all future transactions.

5. Click OK to accept the change.

Add a New Customer

6. Click the New Customer & Job button and choose New Customer.

7. Enter the following information on the Address Info tab:

Name	Karen Douglas
Address	4673 South Stayton Way San Marcos, CA 92069
Phone	760-555-8137
Fax	760-555-8237

8. Enter the following information on the Additional Info tab:

Type	Catering
Terms	Net 15

9. Enter the following information on the Payment Info tab:

Account Number	214

10. Click OK to accept the new record.

11. Create an additional new customer called **Daily Sales**. You will only need to enter the name; no additional information.
    In order to track the food and beverage sales, a "generic" customer needs to be set up.

Delete a Customer Record

12. Single-click Andy Freston to select the name.

13. Choose Edit→Delete Customer:Job from the menu bar.

14. Click OK to confirm the deletion.

15. Close the Customer Center window.

Skill Builder 2.2   Work with Service Items and Sales Forms

In this exercise, you will begin by setting up service items for Susie. Once the items have been created, you will use them in both an invoice and sales receipt.

Create Service Items

Remember, you must create items before you can use them on sales forms. It may seem strange, but a restaurant is technically considered a service business!

1. Open the Item List by choosing Lists→Item List.

2. Click the Item menu button and choose New from the drop-down menu.

3. Create the following service item:

Item Name	Catering
Description	Off-site catering
Rate	[leave this blank--you will fill in for each job]
Account	Catering Sales

4. Click the Next button and create the following service item:

Item Name	Beverages
Description	Daily Beverage Sales
Rate	[leave this blank]
Account	Beverage Sales

5. Click OK to accept the new item and close the window.

6. Close the Item List.

Create an Invoice

7. Open the Create Invoices window by choosing Customers→Create Invoices from the menu bar. Fill in Karen Douglas in the Customer:Job field.

8. Set the date to read 5/3/2010.

9. Choose to use the Intuit Service Invoice Template.

10. Click in the Item column of the invoice and choose Catering as the item.

11. Tap Tab three times and type **$750** in the Rate column.

12. Select "We appreciate your prompt payment" in the Customer Message field.

13. Click Save & Close to record the transaction and close the Create Invoices window.

14. Click No in the QuickBooks Information window about the Payment Interview, if necessary, choosing to not display the message in the future.

Enter a Sales Receipt

15. Open the Enter Sales Receipts window by choosing Customers→Enter Sales Receipts from the menu bar.

16. Choose Daily Sales from the Customer:Job field.

17. Set the date to read 5/5/2010.

18. Enter the receipt as paid with cash.

19. Click the Item column of the sales receipt and choose Food as the item.

20. Enter $**526** as the rate.

21. Click in the Item column below the Food entry, and choose Beverages as the item.

22. Enter $**724** as the rate.

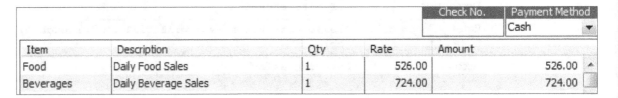

| | | | Check No. | Payment Method |
| | | | | Cash ▼ |

Item	Description	Qty	Rate	Amount
Food	Daily Food Sales	1	526.00	526.00
Beverages	Daily Beverage Sales	1	724.00	724.00

Your sales receipt should look like the figure above.

23. Click Save & Close to record the transaction and close the Enter Sales Receipts window.

Skill Builder 2.3 Deal with Payments and Deposits

In this exercise, you will receive the payment for the invoice you created earlier and you will deposit the payments being held in the Undeposited Funds account.

Receive a Customer's Payment

1. Choose Customers→Receive Payments from the menu bar.

2. Choose Karen Douglas from the Received From field.

3. Enter **$750** for the amount.

4. Set the date to read 5/10/2010.

5. The payment was written on check number **592**.

6. Click Save & Close.

7. Click Don't Ask Again in the Make more money window, if necessary.

Make a Deposit from the Undeposited Funds Account

8. Choose Banking→Make Deposits from the menu bar.
   The Payments to Deposit window will appear since you have payments in the Undeposited Funds account waiting to be deposited.

9. Click the Select All button to mark all payments for deposit, and then click OK.
   Now you will see both of the payments in the Make Deposits window. If you need to replenish your Petty Cash account, you can use this form to receive cash back. You will learn more about Petty Cash accounts in QuickBooks Pro 2010: Level 2.

10. Choose Checking as the account in which you will be depositing these payments.

11. Set the date to read 5/15/2010, click Save & Close to record the transaction, and close the window.

Skill Builder 2.4   Run Customer-Related Reports

In this exercise, you will run three reports for Susie: a customer QuickReport, a customer list report, and a customer transaction detail report.

Create a QuickReport

1. Open the Customer Center.

2. Click Karen Douglas to select it.

3. Click the QuickReport link at the far right of the window.

4. Set the date range to All.
   You will see a report that shows all of the transactions for Esther Busch.

5. Choose Window→Close All from the menu bar.

Create a List Report Using the Menu Bar

6. Choose Reports→Customers & Recievables→Customer Phone List from the menu bar.
   All reports available from the menu bar are also available from the Report Center window.

7. Using your QuickZoom pointer, double-click Karen Douglas.
   QuickBooks will open an Edit Customer window, from where you can make any changes to the customer's information.

8. Choose Window→Close All from the menu bar.

Create a Customer-Related Detail Report

9. Choose Reports→Customers & Receivables→Transaction List by Customer.

10. Type **a** to set the date range to All.
    You will see a report that breaks down all sales transactions by customer.

11. Close the Transaction List by Customer report, choosing not to memorize the report.

12. Choose the appropriate option for your situation:
    - If you are continuing on to Lesson 3 or to the rest of the end-of-lesson exercises, leave QuickBooks open.
    - If you are finished working in QuickBooks, Choose File→Exit from the menu bar.

Assessments

Before you begin these exercises, restore the Assessment 2 portable company file from your file storage location and type in your name as the first word of the filename (e.g., Mary Assessment 2). If you need to review how to open a portable company file, refer to Hands-On 2.1. Click Remind Me Later if the Intuit Account window appears.

Assessment 2.1   Set Up a Customer & Job List

In this exercise, you will set up the Customer & Job List for Island Charters.

1. Open the Customer Center and set up the following customers for Island Charters:
   If you wish, you may explore the Add/Edit Multiple List Entries feature and use it to complete this exercise, although it will be fully introduced in QuickBooks Pro 2010: Level 2.

Customer & Job List field			
Name	Kathy Cushman	Phil McMurray	YMCA Adventures
Address	321 Dockson Road Maury, WA 98069	59135 SW 15th St. Maury, WA 98069	4169 Maury Highway Maury, WA 98069
Phone	206-555-7596	206-555-4426	206-555-8999
Fax	None	None	206-555-8998
Contact Name	Kathy Cushman	Phil McMurray	Cindy Spokes
Type	Personal	Personal	Organization
Terms	Due on Receipt	Due on Receipt	Net 30
Account Number	P105	P107	G235

Assessment 2.2   Work with Customer Transactions

In this exercise, you will bill Island Charters' customers, receive payments, and make deposits.

Record Sales Transactions

1. Cindy Spokes called on **5/07/2010** and reserved a charter for a YMCA group. Invoice the organization for a group charter, net 30.

2. Kathy Cushman stopped by and paid for a half-day charter on **5/10/2010**. Create a sales receipt for her check number **1562** payment of **$89**.

Record Payments and Make Deposits

3. On **5/16/2010**, Mary O'Malley received check number **2463** from YMCA Adventures to be applied toward invoice number 1 for **$500**. Receive the payment into QuickBooks.

4. On **5/17/2010**, Mary O'Malley decides to make a deposit. Create the deposit in QuickBooks, choosing to deposit all of the payments from the undeposited funds account into the checking account.

Assessment 2.3   Work with Customer Reports

In this exercise, you will run various reports for Island Charters.

1. Mary has asked you for a list of her customers and their phone numbers. Create a report in QuickBooks that will answer this question for her.

2. Mary wants to review the transactions that have occurred this month. Run a report that will show her all of the transactions by customer for the month of May.

Critical Thinking

Critical Thinking 2.1   Sort Through the Stack

You have just been hired by Griffin Construction to help the owner catch up with his Quick-Books entries. Open the Critical Thinking 2.1 portable company file from your file storage location and enter the following stack of papers that you found on the owner's desk. Use your best judgment to decide how to handle each item.

- A handwritten invoice dated 5/03/2010 for four hours of drywall work and eight hours of electrical work, billed to Ginger Howell

- A sticky note stuck on a checking deposit slip dated 5/05/2010 for $350 stating, "Received cash for plumbing repair" (Hint: Make a deposit without specifying a customer.)

- A photocopy of check number 576 from Maxwell Consulting for $575 with a note stating that it was deposited on 5/08/2010

- A receipt for three hours of plumbing work paper-clipped to a credit card slip (Hint: Make a deposit with credit card as the payment type, and make sure to indicate the income in the Make Deposits window.)

- A note stating, "Need a way to bill for consulting—new item?" (Hint: Create a new item.)

Critical Thinking 2.2   Work in Magazine Scenario with Two Revenue Sources

You have started a new magazine, The Natural World, and decide to use QuickBooks to keep track of your company's finances. When you began setting up your customers, though, you discovered a little dilemma: Not only do you receive payments from subscribers, but you also receive payments from advertisers. It is important to differentiate these two types of customers (remember, in QuickBooks a customer is someone who pays you money). You also want to be able to track how much advertising each of your sales representatives sells.

Open a QuickBooks file (any will do as you will just be using it to explore a solution to your situation) and come up with a way to track the two types of customers along with how to track advertising sales by rep.

Type your proposed method of handling this dilemma in a word processing program and save it as **Critical Thinking 2.2**. When you are finished, print the document and turn it in to your instructor.

Working with Vendor Transactions

Tracking expenses properly is very important for your financial statements as well as for keeping your vendors happy! A vendor is essentially anyone to whom you pay money. However, this does not include employees. A vendor could be the electric company, the organization to which you pay taxes, a merchandise supplier, or subcontractors you pay to do work for your customers. QuickBooks allows you to produce 1099 tax forms for subcontractors at the end of the year. In this lesson, you will examine the QuickBooks lists, activities, and reports that allow you to effectively deal with vendors.

LESSON OBJECTIVES

After studying this lesson, you will be able to:

- Work with the Vendor List
- Enter and pay bills
- Write checks
- Invoice for billable costs
- Produce vendor and P&L reports
- Produce and work with graphs

Integrative Case Study: Skortis Landscaping

Justin Skortis—the owner of Skortis Landscaping—just began using QuickBooks and needs to create a Vendor List before he can track his expenses by entering bills, paying bills, and writing checks. Once he has established his list of vendors, he will be able to choose them from drop-down lists in the various vendor forms. After he has entered the expenses that match with the income recorded in the last lesson, Justin will be able to create basic vendor and company reports such as standard profit and loss reports.

Justin can access the Vendor List and activities (entering and paying bills) from the Vendor Center. In the following illustration you can see the Vendor Center. In total, there are four centers: Customer, Vendor, Employee, and Report. Centers allow you to view a snapshot of information for a list item; in this case, a snapshot of an individual vendor's information, bills, and payments.

These toolbar buttons allow you to create new list entries, enter new transactions, print a vendor's information, or export information to Microsoft Excel or Word.

The top-right portion of the window displays information for the vendor you have selected on the left, as well as links to reports for the vendor.

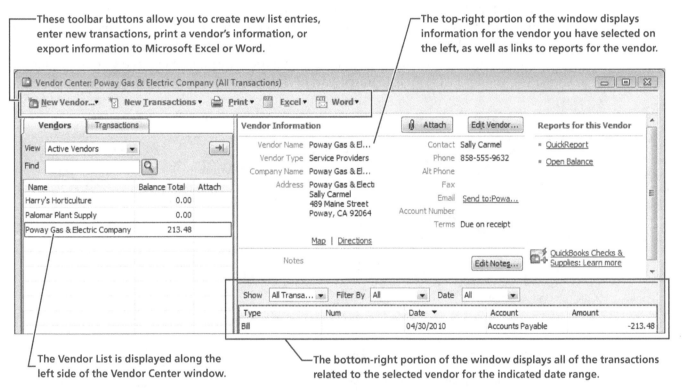

The Vendor List is displayed along the left side of the Vendor Center window.

The bottom-right portion of the window displays all of the transactions related to the selected vendor for the indicated date range.

The Vendor Center window displays the Vendor List as well as a snapshot view of the selected vendor.

Exploring the Vendor List

Remember that QuickBooks uses lists to organize your company's information. Lists allow you to store information that you can easily fill into forms by using drop-down arrows or by just starting to type the entry and letting QuickBooks fill in the rest. Lists comprise the database aspect of QuickBooks. As an option, the Vendor List can be exported to contact management software such as Microsoft Outlook.

In the list section of the Vendor Center you can see the following details:

■ The name of each vendor

■ The balance that you owe each vendor

Each individual vendor record tracks a lot of information that is organized into two tabs: Address Info and Additional Info. For the information that does not already have a field you can create Custom Fields to customize QuickBooks for your unique business (Custom Fields will be introduced in *QuickBooks Pro 2010: Level 2*). Remember, the more information you enter for each vendor, the better prepared you will be later when you learn how to customize reports as you can sort, group, and filter your reports using the information entered into the vendor records. The Vendor List is an integrated part of the Vendor Center.

You can click the Edit Vendor button to make changes to any of the information for the selected vendor.

The integrated Vendor List displays the name of the vendor followed by the balance that is owed the vendor.

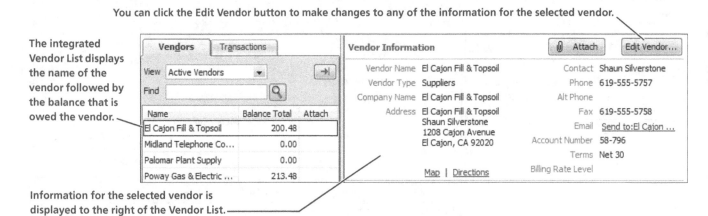

Information for the selected vendor is displayed to the right of the Vendor List.

Managing the Vendor List

The list management techniques that you learned about in Lesson 2, Working with Customer Transactions are very similar for the Vendor List as well as the Employee List. The next three concepts will serve as a review of creating, editing, and deleting Customer & Job, Vendor, and Employee List entries.

Creating a New Vendor

To start entering vendor transactions you must first enter your vendors into the Vendor List. You can enter vendors directly into the list, in the Add/Edit Multiple List Entries window (which you will learn more about in *QuickBooks Pro 2010: Level 2*), or "on the fly" in forms such as Enter Bills and Write Checks and then select Quick Add or Setup from the pop-up window. Remember that subcontractors should be set up as vendors, not as employees.

Editing an Existing Vendor

Once created, the vendor can always be edited through the Vendor Center. The only item that cannot be edited after you have created and saved a new vendor is the opening balance (it must be adjusted through the accounts payable register).

Deleting a Vendor

You can delete a vendor from the Vendor List **as long as you have not used it in a transaction.**

QUICK REFERENCE: MANAGING THE VENDOR LIST	
Task	**Procedure**
Edit an existing vendor	■ Open the Vendor Center.
	■ Double-click the vendor you need to edit.
	■ Make the change(s) in the fields.
	■ Click OK to accept the change(s).
Add a new vendor	■ Open the Vendor Center.
	■ Click the New Vendor Button on the toolbar.
	■ Enter all necessary information.
	■ Click OK to accept the new vendor.
Delete a vendor	■ Open the Vendor Center.
	■ Click the vendor you want to delete.
	■ Choose Edit→Delete Vendor from the menu bar.
	■ Click OK in the box to confirm the deletion.

 Hands-On 3.1   # Manage the Vendor List

In this exercise, you will restore a portable company file and manage your Vendor List.

Open a Portable Company File

The first step is to open QuickBooks and restore the portable company file that you will be using for this lesson.

1. Start QuickBooks.

2. Choose File→Open or Restore Company from the menu bar.

3. Click in the circle to the left of Restore a portable file.

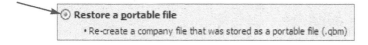

4. Click Next.

5. Navigate to your file storage location and open the QB 2010 Student Files folder.

6. Double-click to select the Hands-On Lesson 3 (Portable) file.

7. Click Next, and then follow these steps to determine where the resulting company file will be located:

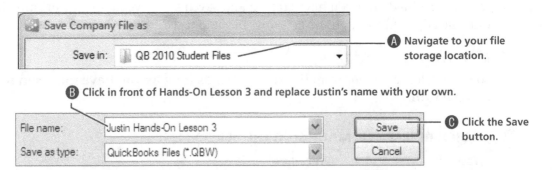

A Navigate to your file storage location.

B Click in front of Hands-On Lesson 3 and replace Justin's name with your own.

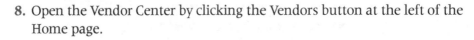

C Click the Save button.

It may take a few moments for the portable company file to restore. After a pause, QuickBooks displays a prompt that the file was restored successfully.

Edit an Existing Vendor

The first step in modifying a vendor record is to open the Vendor Center in order to view the Vendor List.

8. Open the Vendor Center by clicking the Vendors button at the left of the Home page.

9. Double-click Palomar Plant Supply to open it for editing.

!TIP! *When you double-click a record on the Vendor List, QuickBooks opens it for editing. You could also single-click the vendor you wish to open, and then click the Edit Vendor button.*

10. Click in the box to the left of Do not display this message in the future. Click OK in the New Feature window, if necessary.

11. Change the last name of the contact to **Smith**.
Remember, in QuickBooks you can use the same text editing techniques you use in word processing programs. Notice that you will need to change the name in three places.

!TIP! *To select one word, you can double-click the word instead of manually dragging the mouse pointer over it.*

12. Click OK to accept the change.

Add a New Vendor

13. Click the New Vendor button on the toolbar and choose New Vendor from the menu.

14. Notice that your insertion point is in the Vendor Name field. Now, follow these steps to enter the address information for the vendor:

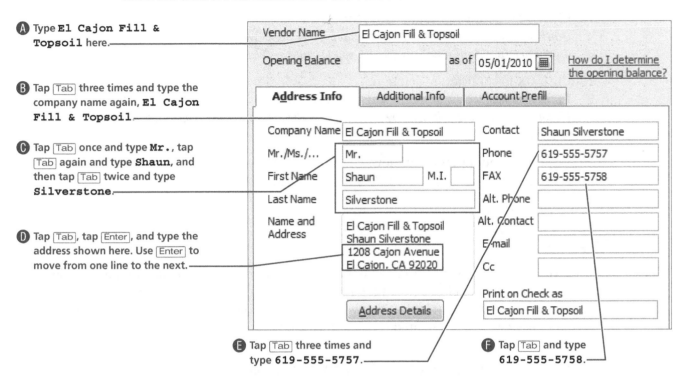

Ⓐ Type **El Cajon Fill & Topsoil** here.

Ⓑ Tap ⌨Tab three times and type the company name again, **El Cajon Fill & Topsoil**.

Ⓒ Tap ⌨Tab once and type **Mr.**, tap ⌨Tab again and type **Shaun**, and then tap ⌨Tab twice and type **Silverstone**.

Ⓓ Tap ⌨Tab, tap ⌨Enter, and type the address shown here. Use ⌨Enter to move from one line to the next.

Ⓔ Tap ⌨Tab three times and type 619-555-5757.

Ⓕ Tap ⌨Tab and type 619-555-5758.

Notice that QuickBooks has filled in the contact name based on what you typed in the name boxes.

15. Follow these steps to add the additional vendor information:

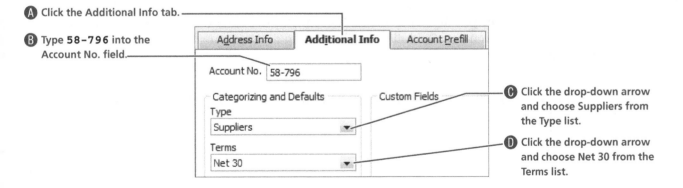

Ⓐ Click the Additional Info tab.

Ⓑ Type **58-796** into the Account No. field.

Ⓒ Click the drop-down arrow and choose Suppliers from the Type list.

Ⓓ Click the drop-down arrow and choose Net 30 from the Terms list.

16. Click OK to complete the new vendor record.

Delete a Vendor

Skortis Landscaping has not purchased anything from Harry's Horticulture, and Harry's has since gone out of business. You will now delete this company from the Vendor List.

17. Single-click the Harry's Horticulture record in the Vendor List to select it.

18. Choose Edit→Delete Vendor from the menu bar.
QuickBooks asks you to confirm the deletion. QuickBooks wants to ensure that you don't delete anything by accident; it will always ask you to confirm deletions.

19. Click OK to confirm the deletion.
In the next step, you will close the Vendor Center window within QuickBooks. Do not click the Close button for the QuickBooks window, as it will exit the program rather than close a center window as you intend!

20. Close the Vendor Center window.

Entering Bills

Once you have set up your initial Vendor List, you can begin to enter spending transactions. In this section you will learn to enter bills and use accounts payable, which is the account credited when bills are entered. When you enter a bill, you **must** specify a vendor because accounts payable will be credited by the transaction.

Entering Vendor Information on Bills

After you select your vendor from the drop-down list at the top of the form, QuickBooks automatically fills the relevant information for that vendor into the appropriate fields on the Enter Bills window. If you wish to enter a bill for a new vendor not yet entered into the Vendor List, QuickBooks will allow you to create the new record "on the fly."

When entering bills you need to decide if the expenditure is for an expense or items that you will add to your inventory. The following illustration displays the primary features of the Enter Bills window.

!NOTE! *In this lesson you will deal only with expenses. You will learn about QuickBooks' inventory features in* QuickBooks Pro 2010: Level 2.

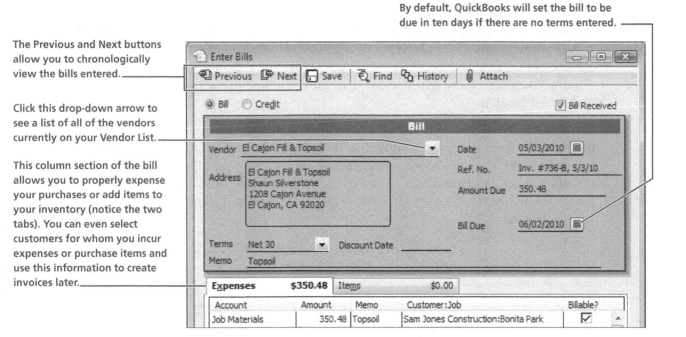

By default, QuickBooks will set the bill to be due in ten days if there are no terms entered.

The Previous and Next buttons allow you to chronologically view the bills entered.

Click this drop-down arrow to see a list of all of the vendors currently on your Vendor List.

This column section of the bill allows you to properly expense your purchases or add items to your inventory (notice the two tabs). You can even select customers for whom you incur expenses or purchase items and use this information to create invoices later.

Making Changes to Vendor Information on Forms

Whenever you make a change to a vendor's information on a form such as the Enter Bills window, QuickBooks asks if you want to make that change permanent. If you choose Yes, QuickBooks will change the vendor's file. If you choose No, the new information will appear only on the current form; the permanent record remains unchanged.

Choosing Accounts to Prefill Information

In QuickBooks, when you set up a vendor, you have the option to choose up to three expense accounts for which information will fill in when you make a payment. By setting up expense account information to be prefilled, you can make it easier and faster to track expenses.

When you enter a vendor's name in the Enter Bills, Write Checks, or Enter Credit Card Charges windows, QuickBooks will fill in the expense account names for you. This allows you to then enter the amounts to be debited to each expense account. By prefilling information, you can make sure that you use the same expense account(s) each time you use a particular vendor. You can always choose to override the default accounts that are filled in by changing them in the individual transaction window. If there are less than three expense accounts for a vendor, just leave the additional account prefill fields blank.

Passing Expenses on to Customers

When you enter a bill, you may be purchasing equipment or supplies for which you wish to pass on the expense to the customer. QuickBooks allows you to easily indicate which expenses are to be billed to a customer by providing a "Billable?" column in the Enter Bills window. Simply ensure that there is a checkmark in the column, and it will be easy to create a customer invoice for the item(s).

The Cost of Goods Sold comprises expenses that are directly related to the manufacture of products or services that the company sells. Some expenses that might be considered Cost of Goods Sold are labor, raw materials, depreciation, and overhead. You cannot pass on the Cost of Goods Sold to a customer (it is instead incorporated into the final price of the product), so make sure that you use the proper type of account (expense) if the costs are to be billed to your customer.

Materials Costs is a COGS account, so you will not see a check box in the Billable? column.

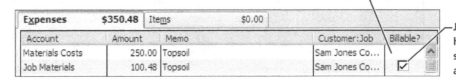

Job Materials, on the other hand, is an expense account, so you can choose to invoice a customer for the amount.

BEHIND THE SCENES

When entering bills, QuickBooks takes care of all of the accounting for you. Here is an illustration of the accounting going on behind the scenes:

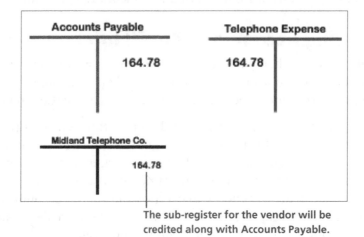

The sub-register for the vendor will be credited along with Accounts Payable.

QUICK REFERENCE: ENTERING BILLS

Task	Procedure
Enter a bill for an existing vendor	■ Open the Enter Bills window. ■ Select a vendor. ■ Enter the amount of the bill. ■ Ensure that the terms are correct. ■ Expense the bill, making sure to select the correct account(s) on the Expenses tab at the bottom of the window. ■ If desired, select a customer to whom you wish to pass the expense. ■ Click OK.
Enter a bill for a vendor not on the Vendor List	■ Open the Enter Bills window. ■ Type the vendor's name into the Vendor field and choose Quick Add or Set Up. ■ Enter the amount of the bill. ■ Enter the terms for this vendor. ■ Expense the bill, making sure to select the correct account(s) on the Expenses tab at the bottom of the window. ■ If desired, select a customer to whom you wish to pass the expense. ■ Click OK.

 ## Hands-On 3.2   Enter Bills

In this exercise, you will enter bills and track expenses.

Before You Begin: Make sure that the Home page is still open. If you need to re-open it, choose Company→Home page from the menu bar.

Enter a Bill for an Existing Vendor

1. Click the Enter Bills task icon in the Vendors area of the Home page.
   The Enter Bills window will open.

2. Click the Vendor drop-down button as shown in the illustration and choose El Cajon Fill & Topsoil.

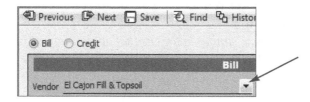

Look at the form and notice that the vendor's terms fill in for you from the underlying list and that the due date is calculated.

3. Tap [Tab] to move to the date field. Then, follow these steps to create a bill for El Cajon Fill & Topsoil:

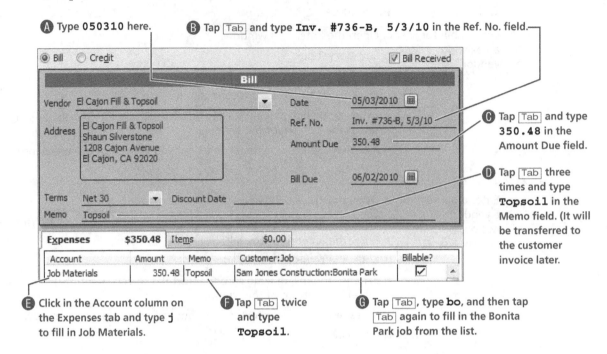

Ⓐ Type **050310** here.

Ⓑ Tap [Tab] and type **Inv. #736-B, 5/3/10** in the Ref. No. field.

Ⓒ Tap [Tab] and type **350.48** in the Amount Due field.

Ⓓ Tap [Tab] three times and type **Topsoil** in the Memo field. (It will be transferred to the customer invoice later.

Ⓔ Click in the Account column on the Expenses tab and type **j** to fill in Job Materials.

Ⓕ Tap [Tab] twice and type **Topsoil**.

Ⓖ Tap [Tab], type **bo**, and then tap [Tab] again to fill in the Bonita Park job from the list.

QuickBooks fills in the Bonita Park job for Sam Jones Construction and moves you to the next column. The last column is the Billable? column. (If a checkmark is displayed, QuickBooks is telling you that you can create an invoice from this bill line item.) You can only pass on expenses, not the cost of good sold, to customers.

4. Click the Save & New button.
QuickBooks records your bill transaction by crediting Accounts Payable and debiting the expense(s) you chose in the Account column (in this case, Job Materials). The Enter Bills window stays open for the next step.

Enter a Bill for a Vendor Not on the Vendor List

When you enter a vendor name that's not on the Vendor List, QuickBooks allows you to add it to the Vendor List.

5. Make sure the insertion point is in the Vendor field at the top of a new bill. Type **Midland Telephone Company** and tap [Tab].
A Vendor Not Found window will appear, similar to the one that appeared when you added a customer "on the fly" in Lesson 2, Working with Customer Transactions.

6. Click Set Up. Then follow these steps to create the new vendor:

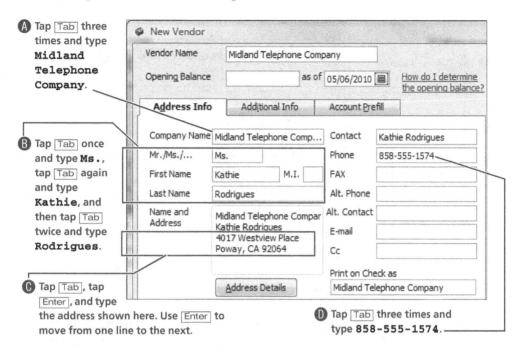

Ⓐ Tap ⌊Tab⌋ three times and type **Midland Telephone Company**.

Ⓑ Tap ⌊Tab⌋ once and type **Ms.**, tap ⌊Tab⌋ again and type **Kathie**, and then tap ⌊Tab⌋ twice and type **Rodrigues**.

Ⓒ Tap ⌊Tab⌋, tap ⌊Enter⌋, and type the address shown here. Use ⌊Enter⌋ to move from one line to the next.

Ⓓ Tap ⌊Tab⌋ three times and type **858-555-1574**.

7. Follow these steps to add the additional vendor information:

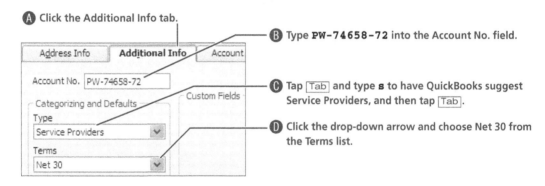

Ⓐ Click the Additional Info tab.

Ⓑ Type **PW-74658-72** into the Account No. field.

Ⓒ Tap ⌊Tab⌋ and type **s** to have QuickBooks suggest Service Providers, and then tap ⌊Tab⌋.

Ⓓ Click the drop-down arrow and choose Net 30 from the Terms list.

8. Follow these steps to set up an account to prefill with this vendor:

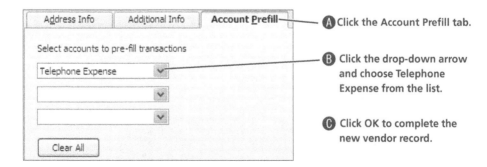

Ⓐ Click the Account Prefill tab.

Ⓑ Click the drop-down arrow and choose Telephone Expense from the list.

Ⓒ Click OK to complete the new vendor record.

9. Follow these steps to complete the bill:

Ⓐ Ensure that 05/03/2010 is the date displayed.

Ⓑ Tap Tab and type **Phone Bill, 4/30/10.**

Ⓒ Tap Tab and type **164.78** as the amount.

Ⓓ Tap Tab three times and type **Phone Bill 4/30/10** in the Memo field.

Ⓔ Tap Tab and ensure that *Telephone Expense* is displayed.

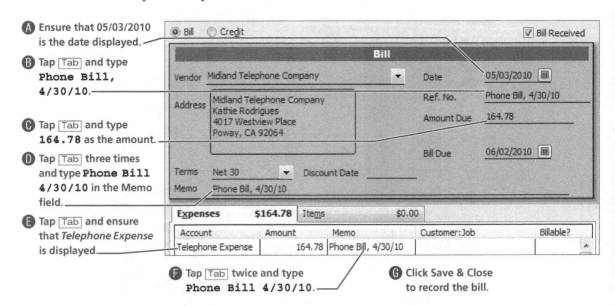

Ⓕ Tap Tab twice and type **Phone Bill 4/30/10.**

Ⓖ Click Save & Close to record the bill.

⚠ **!TIP!** *Rather than typing the information for the reference number and memo fields three times, you can drag to select the information in the Ref. No. field, copy it, and then paste it in the two Memo fields.*

Paying Bills

Once you have entered your bills, you will need to pay them in a timely manner. In Quick-Books you use the Pay Bills window to debit accounts payable. The other half of the equation (the account that will be credited) depends on the account from which you withdraw funds (or charge in the case of bill payment by credit card). The Pay Bills window shows all bills due in chronological order by due date. If you wish, you can choose Due On or Before and set a date by which to arrange the list.

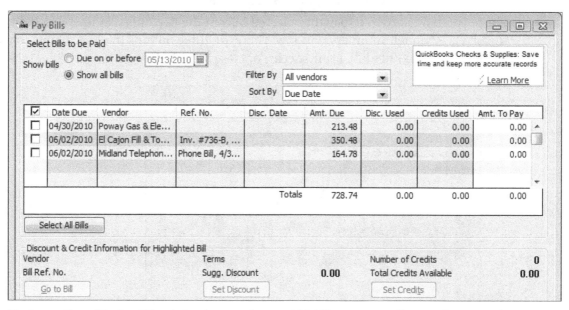

The top portion of the Pay Bills window lets you choose which bills to pay as well as any discount and credit information for the selected bill.

⚠️ **WARNING!** *When you have used the Enter Bills window, make sure you use the Pay Bills window to issue the payment, **not** the Write Checks window! If you use the Write Checks window you will expense the purchase twice and not "clear out" the entry in the accounts payable register.*

Payment Details

At the bottom of the Pay Bills window, you must make three important choices regarding your payment: Payment Method, Payment Account, and Payment Date.

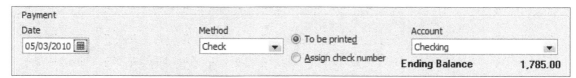

QuickBooks allows you to choose the payment options for each bill.

■ **Payment Method**—You can choose how you will pay the bill. If you choose to pay by check, you must select whether you will print the check or write it by hand. You will learn how to print checks in the Writing Checks section. You can also choose to pay your bill by credit card. In order to pay by credit card you must have a credit card account set up. Then you can choose it from the Payment Method drop-down list.

- **Payment Account**—You can select to pay the bill from any bank account you have created. When you select an account, QuickBooks will show you the ending balance for the account so you can ensure you have enough money to pay the bill. Make sure you select the proper account, as it will be credited behind the scenes!

- **Payment Date**—Make sure you select the date you want the payment to be reflected in your bank and accounts payable accounts.

The Payment Summary Window

Once you have chosen to pay the selected bills in the Pay Bills window, QuickBooks will display a Payment Summary window. There are three options made available to you from this window: pay another bill, print checks, or close the window.

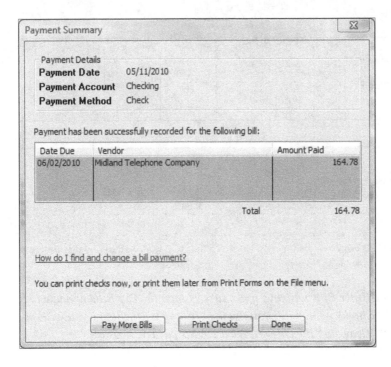

The Payment Summary window summarizes all of the bills that you just recorded and provides you with options for your next step.

BEHIND THE SCENES

Let's look at the accounting scenario that results when you pay bills:

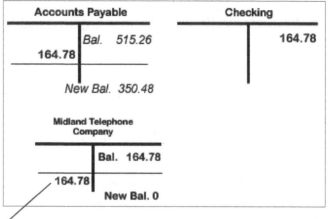

QuickBooks debits the sub-register for the vendor along with Accounts Payable.

QUICK REFERENCE: PAYING BILLS

Task	Procedure
Pay a bill	■ Open the Pay Bills window.
	■ If you don't see the bill you want to pay, click the circle to the left of the Show All Bills option.
	■ Select the bill you want to pay.
	■ Select the account from which you wish to make the payment, along with the payment method and date.
	■ Click Pay & Close or Pay & New depending on whether you have to pay other bills.
Pay a partial amount on a bill	■ Open the Pay Bills window.
	■ If you don't see the bill you want to pay, click the circle to the left of the Show All Bills option.
	■ Select the bill you want to pay.
	■ Click and drag over the amount displayed in the Amt. to Pay column and type the amount you want to pay.
	■ Select the account from which you wish to make the payment, along with the payment method and date.
	■ Click Pay & Close or Pay & New depending on whether you have to pay other bills.

In this exercise, you will pay the bills that have been entered.

Before you begin: Make sure that the Home page is still open. If you need to re-open it, choose Company→Home Page from the menu bar.

Pay a Bill in Its Entirety

Justin is ready to pay the telephone bill so he will complete the task by using the Pay Bills window.

1. Click the Pay Bills task icon on the Home page.
   The Pay Bills window will open with the Show All Bills option selected at the top of the window.

2. Follow these steps to pay the telephone bill:

A Click in the box beside the bill due for Midland Telephone. QuickBooks displays a checkmark to indicate that the bill is to be paid.

B Ensure that Check is chosen as the Payment Method.

C Click the calendar button in the Payment Date field and choose 5/11/10.

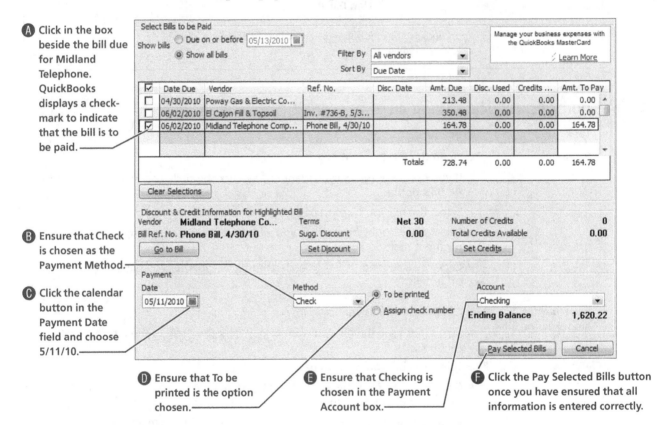

D Ensure that To be printed is the option chosen.

E Ensure that Checking is chosen in the Payment Account box.

F Click the Pay Selected Bills button once you have ensured that all information is entered correctly.

QuickBooks displays a Payment Summary window.

3. Click Pay More Bills in the Payment Summary window.

Pay a Partial Amount on a Bill

Now Justin will make a partial payment of $150 on the El Cajon Fill & Topsoil bill for $350.48.

4. Follow these steps to complete the Pay Bills window:

A Click to place a checkmark for the El Cajon Fill & Topsoil bill.

B Click anywhere within the Payment Date field and tap the ⊞ key until the date reads 05/13/2010.

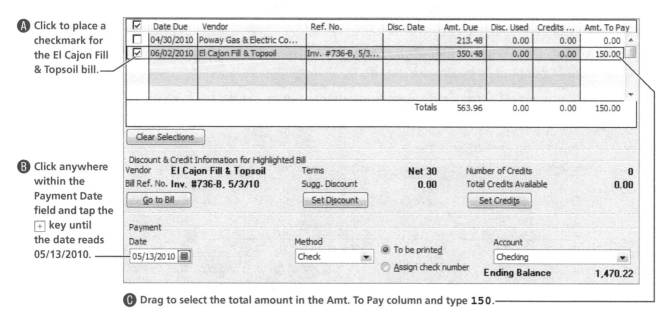

C Drag to select the total amount in the Amt. To Pay column and type **150**.

Once you have the total bill amount selected, you can type the amount you are going to pay. Notice that the Bill Ref. No. information you typed in the Enter Bills window is displayed in the Discount & Credit Information for Highlighted Bill section of the Pay Bills window.

5. Click the Pay Selected Bills button to complete the transaction.

6. Click Pay More Bills in the Payment Summary window.
   Take a look at the current bills to be paid. Notice that the bill for El Cajon Fill & Topsoil is still on the list, but only for the remaining amount due ($200.48).

7. Taking care not to close the QuickBooks program window, close the Pay Bills window.
   The Pay Bills window will close, and you will see the Home page displayed.

Writing Checks

If you are using the cash basis of accounting, you do not have to use the enter bills and pay bills features of QuickBooks, even though these are useful features for managing cash flow. You can simply write a check to pay for your expenditures when they are due and expense them properly.

As with the Pay Bills window, you must decide from which account to issue the check and whether to print or handwrite the check.

The following illustration displays primary features of the Write Checks window:

You can choose from which account you wish to write the check in this field (if you have multiple bank accounts). ⟍

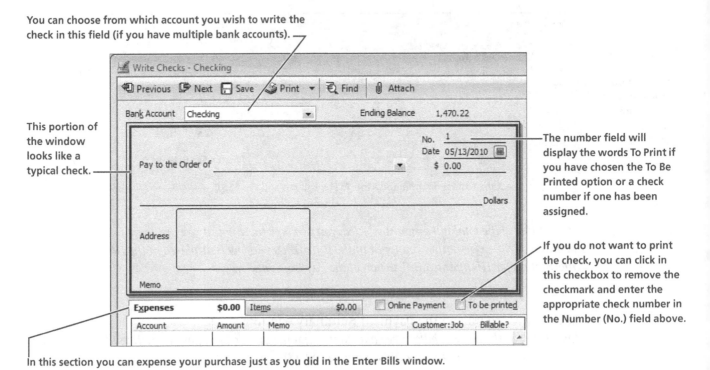

This portion of the window looks like a typical check.

The number field will display the words To Print if you have chosen the To Be Printed option or a check number if one has been assigned.

If you do not want to print the check, you can click in this checkbox to remove the checkmark and enter the appropriate check number in the Number (No.) field above.

In this section you can expense your purchase just as you did in the Enter Bills window. You can also choose to pass on expenses to customers or jobs.

Printing Checks

When you choose to print your checks in the Pay Bills and Write Checks windows, QuickBooks will "hold" all of them in a queue until you are ready to print a batch of checks. You can print a batch of checks from the menu bar. Or, you can click the Print Checks task icon in the Banking area of the Home page.

When you choose to print checks, you will see the Select Checks to Print window displayed. You can choose exactly which checks to print in your batch from this window.

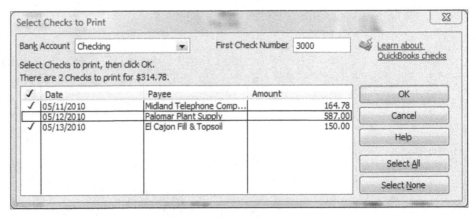

Print Checks - Confirmation ☒

If your checks printed correctly, click OK.

What if my checks printed in reverse order?

If you need to reprint any checks, select them and click OK. Then return to the Select Checks to Print window to reprint them.

Reprint	Check No.	Payee	Amount
	3000	Midland Telephone Company	164.78
	3001	El Cajon Fill & Topsoil	150.00

Once you have sent a batch of checks to the printer, you will see a confirmation window where you have an opportunity to reprint any checks that did not print correctly.

BEHIND THE SCENES

The behind the scenes accounting that occurs when you write a check is a hybrid of the two previous transactions (Enter Bills and Pay Bills), with the elimination of Accounts Payable, the middle-man:

Checking		Job Materials Expense	
	587	587	

QUICK REFERENCE: WRITING CHECKS

Task	Procedure
Write a check to be printed	■ Open the Write Checks window. ■ Select or type the vendor in the Pay to the Order Of field. ■ Type the amount of the check. ■ Ensure there is a checkmark in the To Be Printed checkbox. ■ Select the proper expense account(s) on the Expenses tab. ■ Select a customer if you want to pass on the expense. ■ Click Save & Close or Save & New depending on whether you have to produce additional checks.
Record a handwritten check	■ Open the Write Checks window. ■ Select or type the vendor in the Pay to the Order Of field. ■ Type the amount of the check. ■ Ensure there is **no** checkmark in the To Be Printed checkbox. ■ Select the proper expense account(s) on the Expenses tab. ■ Select a customer if you want to pass on the expense. ■ Click Save & Close or Save & New depending on whether you have to produce additional checks.
Print a batch of checks	■ Select File→Print Forms→Checks from the menu bar. ■ Select the checks you wish to print from the Select Checks to Print window and click OK. ■ Select the correct options in the Print Checks window and click OK.

In this exercise, Justin will pay for expenses with both printed and handwritten checks.

Write a Check to Be Printed for an Expense

1. Click the Write Checks task icon in the Banking area of the Home page.
   The Write Checks window opens with the insertion point in the Bank Account field and the default bank account (in this case, Checking) selected.

2. Tap ⌈Tab⌉ twice. Then, follow these steps to complete the check:

Ⓐ Type **051210** in the Date field.

Ⓑ Tap ⌈Tab⌉ and type **p**. Notice that QuickBooks selects Palomar Plant Supply as the vendor.

Ⓒ Tap ⌈Tab⌉ and type **587** as the amount.

Ⓓ Tap ⌈Tab⌉ four times, and then tap the ⌈Spacebar⌉ to select for the check to be printed.

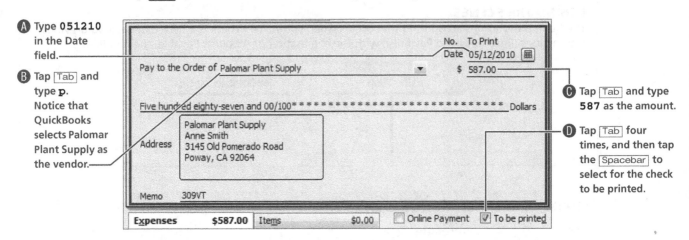

!TIP! *If you tap ⌈Spacebar⌉ when a checkbox is selected, it will either check or uncheck the box for you (toggling between the options).*

Ⓔ Tap ⌈Tab⌉ and type **j** in the Account column to fill in Job Materials.

Ⓕ Tap ⌈Tab⌉ and type **550**.

Ⓖ Tap ⌈Tab⌉ twice and type **bo** for the Bonita Park job to fill in.

Ⓗ Tap ⌈Tab⌉ twice and type **po** to fill in Postage & Delivery.

Ⓘ Tap ⌈Tab⌉ three times and type **bo** for the Bonita Park job.

Ⓙ Tap ⌈Tab⌉ to accept the Customer:Job, and it will be assigned as billable.

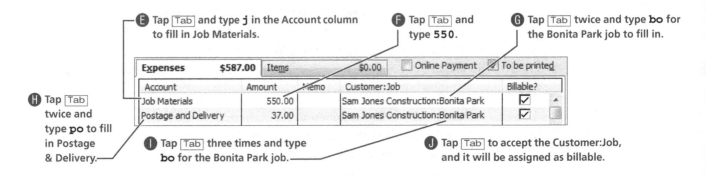

Notice that the expenditure was split between multiple expense accounts and that QuickBooks filled in the amount remaining after you entered the first line. If a customer has multiple jobs, it is important that you select the correct job and not just the correct customer!

3. Click Save & New to record this check and leave the Write Checks window open.

Record a Handwritten Check

You may not always be at your computer when you wish to write a check. In this situation, Justin has taken his checkbook shopping and needs to record the handwritten check.

4. Click to remove the checkmark from the To Be Printed box.

Notice that once you remove the checkmark, the next check number appears in the No. field at the top of the check. If this number is not correct, you can select and replace it.

5. Follow these steps to record the handwritten check:

Ⓐ Click after the 1 and type **001**.

Ⓑ Tap Tab and use the + key to change the date to 5/16/2010.

Ⓒ Tap Tab and type **Chaparral Office Supply**.

Ⓓ Tap Tab and choose to Quick Add the new vendor.

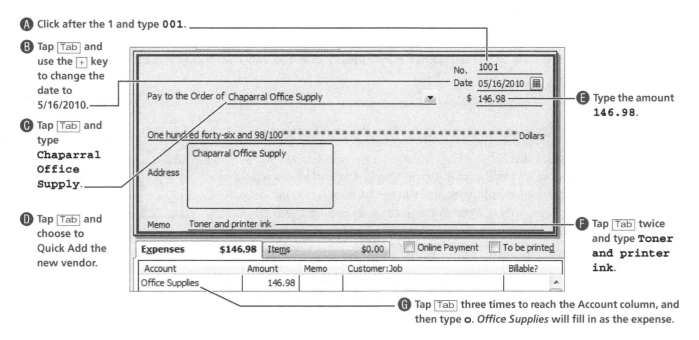

Ⓔ Type the amount **146.98**.

Ⓕ Tap Tab twice and type **Toner and printer ink**.

Ⓖ Tap Tab three times to reach the Account column, and then type **o**. *Office Supplies* will fill in as the expense.

6. Click the Save & Close button to complete the transaction.

Print a Batch of Checks

Once you have indicated that checks are to be printed, you need to issue a separate command to print them.

7. Click the Print Checks task icon in the Banking area of the Home page.
   The Select Checks to Print window will appear.

⚠ **NOTE!** *If you don't see the Print Checks task icon, use the sizing arrows or the maximize button to make the Home page larger.*

8. Tap ⌷Tab⌷ and type **3000** as the first check number.
   By default, all of the checks will be selected.

9. Click the Palomar Plant Supply check to deselect it.

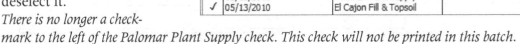

✓	Date	Payee	Amount
✓	05/11/2010	Midland Telephone Comp...	164.78
	05/12/2010	Palomar Plant Supply	587.00
✓	05/13/2010	El Cajon Fill & Topsoil	150.00

   There is no longer a checkmark to the left of the Palomar Plant Supply check. This check will not be printed in this batch.

10. Click OK.
    The Print Checks window will appear.

11. Ensure that Voucher is chosen as the check style.

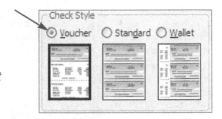

12. Click Print.
    QuickBooks will display a Print Checks-Confirmation window. Here you have the opportunity to reprint any checks that did not print correctly or to troubleshoot the order in which your checks printed.

13. Click OK in the Print Checks-Confirmation window.

Invoicing for Billable Costs

As you may recall, you decided to pass on expenses for the Bonita Park job to Sam Jones Construction in the previous section. Now you will learn how to create an invoice based on a job that has outstanding billable costs. Once you create the invoice from the billable costs, you can add additional expenses as well.

After you have indicated that an expense is to be passed on to a customer in the Write Checks or Enter Bills window, you will be prompted to indicate whether you wish to pass on the billable time or costs each time you create an invoice for the customer (until all expenses have been passed on). When you see the Billable Time/Costs window, you have the opportunity to either add the outstanding billable time or costs to the invoice or exclude them to be invoiced at a later date. There is also an option to set your preference for this feature in the window.

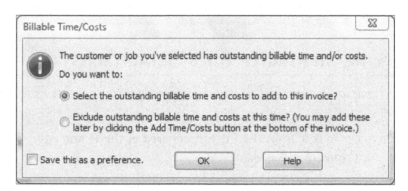

The Billable Time/Costs window will appear every time you choose to create an invoice for a customer who has outstanding billable time or costs. If you typically choose one option over another, you may want to set the preference so that your most commonly selected option appears each time you have billable time or costs.

BEHIND THE SCENES
The accounting involved in this transaction will reverse the debiting of the expense accounts (by crediting them) that occurred in the Enter Bills or Write Checks window since you are passing the expense on to the customer.

Freight and Delivery Expense		Job Materials Expense	
	37		900.48

Accounts receivable will be debited for the expenses passed on to the customer, and an income account will be credited for any additional line items added to the invoice. Note that the total debits ($1,937.48) equals the total credits ($37+900.48+1000=$1.937.48) in this transaction.

Accounts Receivable		Installation Income	
1937.48			1000

QUICK REFERENCE: INVOICING FOR BILLABLE COSTS

Task	Procedure
Create an invoice based on billable costs	■ Open the Create Invoices window.
	■ Click the Customer:Job field drop-down arrow and choose the customer or job for whom you wish to create the invoice.
	■ Make your selection, and then click OK in the Billable Time/Costs window.
	■ Click on the tab for the type of billable costs you wish to pass on.
	■ Select the billable costs to pass on by clicking in the checkmark column or by clicking Select All.
	■ Click on OK to accept the billable costs and move on to the Create Invoices window.
	■ Complete the rest of the invoice as describe in the previous lesson.

 Hands-On 3.5   Create an Invoice for Billable Costs

In this exercise, you will create an invoice based on expenses incurred for Sam Jones Construction's Bonita Park job.

1. Click the Create Invoices task icon in the Customers area of the Home page. *QuickBooks displays the Create Invoices window.*

2. Using the drop-down arrow, choose Sam Jones Construction's Bonita Park job from the Customer:Job list.

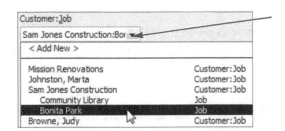

QuickBooks displays the following prompt because you have billable costs for this job:

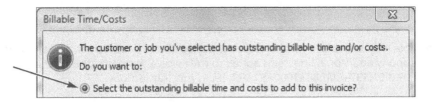

3. Ensure that "Select the outstanding billable time and costs to add to this invoice?" is selected in the Billable Time/Costs window, and then click OK to reach the Choose Billable Time and Costs window.

4. Follow these steps to invoice for the billable costs:

A Click the Expenses tab at the top of the window.

B Click the Select All button to pass on all of the displayed costs to Sam Jones Construction.

C Click OK.

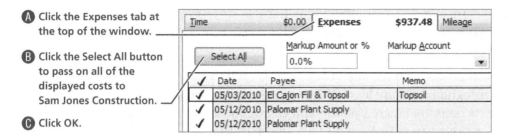

QuickBooks displays the Create Invoices window with the reimbursable expenses grouped as an item (notice that the item name is Reimb Group and the individual costs are indented below the item). If you can't see all of the lines of individual expenses, make your Create Invoices window larger.

Complete the Invoice Form

Now that you have chosen the billable expenses, you will complete and save the transaction.

5. Follow these steps to complete the invoice (you may need to make the window larger in order to see all of the entries):

A Look in the Description column to the left of the $350.48 entry. *Topsoil* was filled in from the Memo field on the bill.

B Click in the Description column to the left of the $37.00 entry, type **Delivery Charge,** and tap the ⬇ key.

C Type **Shrubs and Trees** and tap Alt + m.

D Type **w** and tap Tab to choose "We appreciate your prompt payment" for the Customer Message field.

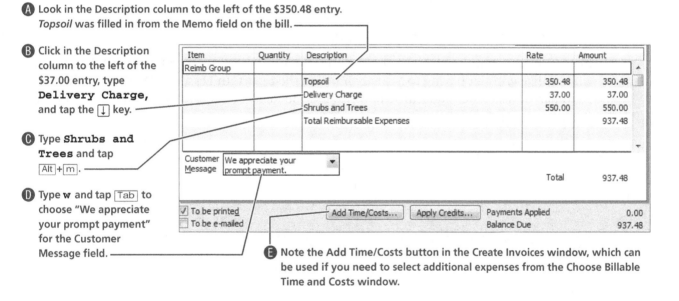

E Note the Add Time/Costs button in the Create Invoices window, which can be used if you need to select additional expenses from the Choose Billable Time and Costs window.

You can add your own descriptions on your customer's invoice if they do not fill in from the Memo field on the original bill or check. It's recommended that you enter detailed information into the Memo field when you enter bills or write checks because you have it handy at that point.

 TIP! *When you tap Alt along with an underlined letter from the screen (such as m for Customer Message), you will be moved to that field to input information.*

6. Click the Save & Close button to complete the transaction.

7. Close the Get More from QuickBooks window, if necessary.
   QuickBooks records your invoice and closes the window.

Producing Vendor and P&L Reports

You learned in Lesson 2, Working with Customer Transactions that there are many preset reports you can run for customer-related transactions. The same is true for vendor- and company-related transactions.

Now that you have recorded both income and expenses for May you will be able to run a meaningful profit and loss (P&L) report. It is important to make sure all income and expense transactions are entered so that you ensure income is matched to expenses for the period you are reporting. A P&L is a financial report that can be found in the Company & Financial category of the Report Center window. The P&L report will reflect all transactions that have affected income and expense accounts.

If you wish to see all transactions grouped by vendor, there are two different reports you can run. The Vendor Balance Detail report (found in the Vendors & Payables category) shows only those transactions affecting Accounts Payable (transactions entered and paid as "bills"). The Expense by Vendor reports (both summary and detail, found in the Company & Financial category) show transactions made by all payment methods.

!NOTE! *See the Working with Reports Quick Reference table in Lesson 2 (page 55) for steps on producing and printing QuickBooks reports.*

View Sample Report Images

An additional feature available in the Report Center is the ability for you to view what a report will look like without having to actually produce the report. In Lesson 2, Working with Customer Transactions, you learned how to use the Report Center to display a report. You can also use it to preview sample reports quickly.

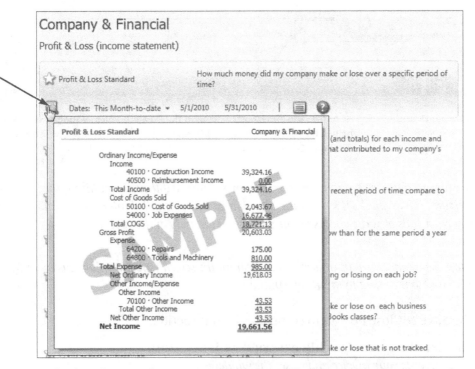

Notice that when you place your mouse pointer over the View sample report button, the sample report is displayed for you. To longer view the report, simply move your mouse pointer away from the button.

In this exercise, you will help Justin create various vendor and profit and loss reports.

Create a Vendor Balance Detail Report

Justin wants to run a report to see exactly what he owes his vendors.

1. Click the Report Center button on the icon bar.
   The report shows only those transactions that affected the accounts payable account.
   Notice that the check written to Chaparral Office Supply is not listed since it didn't affect Accounts Payable.

2. Follow these steps to create a Vendor Balance Detail report:

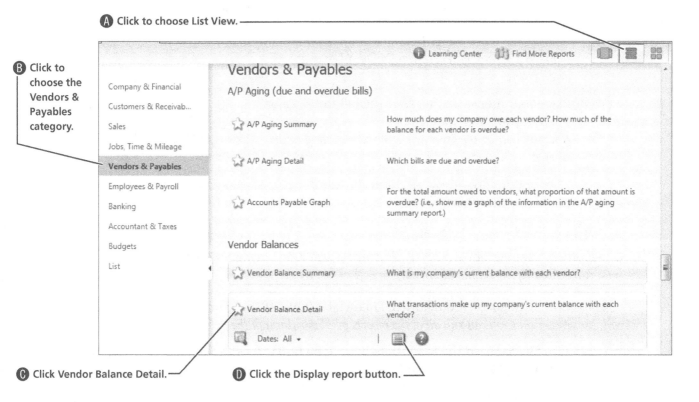

Ⓐ Click to choose List View.

Ⓑ Click to choose the Vendors & Payables category.

Ⓒ Click Vendor Balance Detail.

Ⓓ Click the Display report button.

   QuickBooks will display the Vendor Balance Detail report, which shows only those transactions that affected the Accounts Payable account. Notice that the check written to Chaparral Office Supply is not listed; it didn't affect Accounts Payable.

3. Close the Vendor Balance Detail report, leaving the Report Center open.

Preview and Create a Vendor-Related Summary Report

You can preview what data a report will contain before you create it. The Report Center should still be open. If it is not, choose Reports→Report Center from the menu bar.

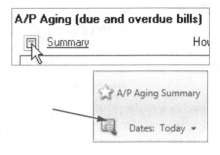

4. Place your mouse pointer over the View sample report button and take a look at the sample report displayed.

5. Click the Display report button.

6. Tap ⓐ to set the date range to All.

7. Place your mouse pointer over the amount for El Cajon Fill & Topsoil until you see the zoom pointer as shown and double-click.
   You will see a report that displays the A/P aging details for El Cajon Fill & Topsoil. When you quick zoom on a summary report, you will be taken to a detail report.

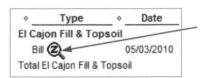

8. Place your mouse pointer over the bill for El Cajon Fill & Topsoil and double-click.
   Now you will see the form where the bill was originally entered.

9. Choose Window→Close All from the menu bar. Click No when asked if you want to memorize the report.

Run a Profit and Loss Report

Justin is now interested in seeing if his company had a net income or net loss for the month of May. He will run a P&L report to find his answer.

10. Choose Reports→Company & Financial→Profit & Loss Standard from the menu bar.
    Notice that you can run all of the reports available through the Report Center via the menu bar as well.

11. Tap [Tab] to reach the From Date field. Type **050110** as the starting date, tap the [Tab] key, and type **053110** as the ending date.

12. Tap the [Tab] key.
    You will see a report that shows your total income and expenses for the time period along with the resulting net income (or loss). Your report should match the illustration at right. Notice that QuickBooks changes the date range to Custom on the toolbar—QuickBooks gives you the option to set the exact date range you desire in your reports.

13. Close the Profit & Loss report, choosing not to memorize the report.

Working with QuickBooks Graphs

QuickBooks provides several graphs along with the preset reports. QuickBooks graphs are accessible through the Reports option on the menu bar or through the Report Center.

Types of QuickBooks Graphs

Following are the six graphs provided by QuickBooks. If you can't find a graph that suits your needs, you always have the option to export a report to Excel and use Excel charting features to create additional charts and graphs.

The graphs provided in QuickBooks include the following:

- Income and Expense

- Net Worth

- Accounts Receivable

- Sales

- Accounts Payable

- Budget vs. Actual

The Graph Toolbar

The Graph toolbar will display different buttons depending on which graph you have created. Once you have created your graph, you can use the Graph toolbar to do a variety of tasks such as the following:

- Customize your graph by date

- Choose whether to view your data by account, customer, or class

- View your next group of information

- Print your graph

- Refresh the data contained within your graph (if you have made changes to your data since the graph was created)

For some graphs, there are also buttons at the bottom of the window that allow you to choose how to view the pie chart data at the bottom of the window (e.g., by Income or by Expense).

QuickZooming with Graphs

The QuickZoom feature you used in previous lessons for reports is also available with graphs. You simply double-click on a portion of a graph (when you see the QuickZoom pointer) to zoom in and see where the data comes from.

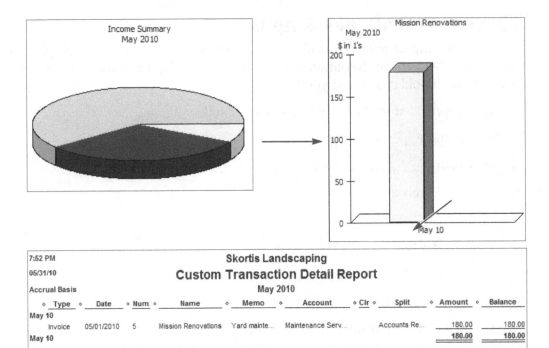

Notice that when you QuickZoom on a pie chart, you see a bar graph; when you QuickZoom on a bar graph, you see a report showing where the data originated.

QR

QUICK REFERENCE: CREATING GRAPHS	
Task	**Procedure**
Run an income and expense graph	Choose Reports→Company & Financial→Income and Expense Graph from the menu bar.
Run a sales graph	Choose Reports→Sales→Sales Graph from the menu bar.

 Hands-On 3.7   Create QuickBooks Graphs

In this exercise, you will use the QuickBooks graphing feature to help Justin get a graphic look at Skortis Landscaping's financial picture.

Create an Income and Expense Graph

To see a comparison of income and expenses, you will create an income and expense graph for Justin.

1. Choose Reports→Company & Financial→Income & Expense Graph.

2. Follow these steps to set the date range:

Ⓐ **Click the Dates button at the far left of the toolbar.**

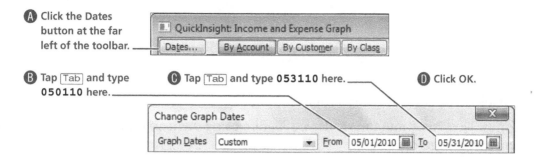

Ⓑ **Tap** `Tab` **and type 050110 here.**

Ⓒ **Tap** `Tab` **and type 053110 here.**

Ⓓ **Click OK.**

You will see a bar graph at the top that displays sales by account and a pie chart at the bottom that shows the expenses broken down by account.

3. Click the By Customer button on the top toolbar.
Notice that there is no chart at the bottom of the window because expenses are not categorized by customer.

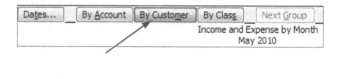

4. Click the Income button at the bottom of the window.
The pie chart now displays the income broken down by customer for the month of May.

5. Close the QuickInsight: Income and Expense Graph window.

Create a Sales Graph

Justin wants to know which items brought in the greatest revenue. Now you will create a sales graph for him.

6. Choose Reports→Sales→Sales Graph from the menu bar.

7. Click the Dates button on the graph toolbar.

8. Tap `Tab` and type **050110**.

9. Tap `Tab` and type **053110**.

10. Click OK to view the graph.
The pie chart displays the percentage of sales by item.

11. Click and hold the right mouse button over the pie slice that represents Installation income.
When you click and hold the right mouse button over a section of the graph, a box appears displaying the dollar amount that the section represents.

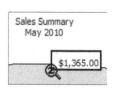

12. Choose the appropriate option for your situation:

■ If you are continuing on to Lesson 4 or to the end-of-lesson exercises, leave QuickBooks open and complete the Concepts Review section.

■ If you are finished working in QuickBooks, Choose File→Exit from the menu bar.

Concepts Review

True/False Questions

1. In QuickBooks, subcontractors are considered vendors.   TRUE   FALSE

2. Vendors must be entered into the Vendor List before using them on forms; you cannot enter them "on the fly."   TRUE   FALSE

3. You can delete a vendor from the Vendor List as long as it has been used less than ten times in transactions.   TRUE   FALSE

4. When you use the Enter Bills window in QuickBooks, you must specify a vendor.   TRUE   FALSE

5. When using the Enter Bills window, accounts payable is debited.   TRUE   FALSE

6. The Pay Bills window shows all bills due in chronological order by due date.   TRUE   FALSE

7. You have to use the Enter Bills and Pay Bills features to account for expenses; you cannot just write a check.   TRUE   FALSE

8. You can create invoices based on outstanding billable costs that you entered into the Enter Bills window.   TRUE   FALSE

9. If you use the cash basis of accounting, you must use the Write Checks window when paying bills, not the Enter Bills window.   TRUE   FALSE

10. You only have to enter your income to create an accurate P&L report.   TRUE   FALSE

Multiple Choice Questions

1. When you open the Vendor Center, what information is not displayed?
   a. Vendor name
   b. Whether notes have been created for the vendor
   c. The balance you owe the vendor
   d. Your credit limit with the vendor

2. When you pay a bill, what account is debited?
   a. Accounts Payable
   b. Checking
   c. Accounts Receivable
   d. Telephone Expense

3. Which of the following is not a list or database task performed with the Vendor List?
   a. Edit a vendor's information
   b. Create a new vendor
   c. Enter a bill for a vendor
   d. Delete a vendor

4. What will prevent you from the ability to delete a vendor record from the Vendor List?
   a. You have previously edited the vendor's information.
   b. You entered an account number for the vendor.
   c. You used the vendor in a transaction.
   d. All of the above

Skill Builders

Before you begin these exercises, restore the Skill Builder 3 portable company file from your file storage location, placing your name as the first word in the filename. If you need to review how to restore a portable company file, follow steps 1–7 in Hands-On 3.1.

Skill Builder 3.1 Manage the Vendor List

In this exercise, you will work with the Vendor List for The Tea Shoppe at the Lake. You will edit an existing vendor, create a new vendor, and delete a vendor.

Edit a Vendor Record

1. Open the Vendor Center by choosing Vendors→Vendor Center from the menu bar.

2. Double-click Valley Insurance Company to open it for editing.

3. Change the vendor's name to **Vista Insurance Company**.
   You will have to change the name in four separate places. This new name will be reflected in all transactions that deal with this vendor—past and present.

4. Click OK to accept the change.

Add a New Vendor

5. Click the New Vendor button, and then choose New Vendor.

6. Enter the following information to create a new vendor:

Company Name	**Palomar Property Management**
Contact Name	**Ms. Wilma Klement**
Address	**525 E. San Marcos Road** **San Marcos, CA 92069**
Phone	**760-555-9438**
Fax	**760-555-9455**
Terms	**Net 30**
Account #	**84-976**

7. Click OK to accept the new vendor record.

Delete a Vendor

8. Click Carlsbad Restaurant Supply to select it.

9. Choose Edit→Delete Vendor from the menu bar.

10. Click OK to confirm the deletion, and then close the Vendor Center window.

Skill Builder 3.2   Enter and Pay Bills

In this exercise, you will enter and pay a bill for Susie.

Enter a Bill

1. Open the Enter Bills window by choosing Vendors→Enter Bills from the menu bar.

2. Click the drop-down arrow and choose Palomar Property Management as the Vendor.

3. Set the date to **5/01/2010**.

4. Type **$1895** for the amount.

5. Choose Rent Expense as the account.

6. Type **June Rent** as the memo and reference number.

7. Click the Save & Close button to enter the transaction and close the window.

Pay a Bill

8. Open the Pay Bills window by choosing Vendors→Pay Bills from the menu bar.

9. Choose the bill for Palomar Property Management by clicking to the left of it in the checkbox.

10. Set the date to **5/5/10**.

11. Click Pay Selected Bills to record the payment and close the window.

12. Click Done in the Payment Summary Window.

Skill Builder 3.3   Write and Print Checks

In this exercise, you will write a check for an expense and print the checks you have created.

Use the Write Checks Window to Enter an Expense

1. Open the Write Checks window by choosing Banking→Write Checks from the menu bar.

2. Set the check number to **1900**.

3. Set the date to **5/06/2010**.

4. Type **San Diego County** into the Pay to the Order Of field and choose to Quick Add it to the Vendor List.

5. Type **$125** as the amount and **Business License** as the memo.

6. Select Business Licenses and Permits as the account.

7. Choose Save & Close to accept the transaction and close the window.

Print a Batch of Checks

8. Choose File→Print Forms→Checks from the menu bar.
   Notice that, by default, QuickBooks selects all checks; you can change this if you need to.

9. Ensure that Checking is the bank account chosen. Then type **1000** as the first check number.

10. Click OK to move to the Print Checks window.
    At this point you can verify that the correct printer and check style are selected. For exercise purposes, you will not print the checks.

11. Click Cancel on both windows.

Skill Builder 3.4   Create Reports

In this exercise, you will run a vendor report and a P&L report for The Tea Shoppe.

Run a Vendor-Related Report

1. Choose Reports→Vendors & Payables→Transaction List by Vendor from the menu bar.

2. Set the date range to All.
   This report will give Susie a snapshot of all recorded vendor transactions.

3. Choose Window→Close All from the menu bar.
   When QuickBooks asks if you want to memorize the report, choose No.

Run a Company (P&L) Report

4. Choose Reports→Company & Financial→Profit & Loss Standard.

5. Set the date range to All.
   This report is based on just a few transactions and therefore is not very realistic. What is important is for you to understand what the report will tell you and how to run it.

6. Choose Window→Close All from the menu bar. Do not memorize the report.

7. Choose the appropriate option for your situation:
   - If you are continuing on to Lesson 4 or to the rest of the end-of-lesson exercises, leave QuickBooks open.
   - If you are finished working in QuickBooks, Choose File→Exit from the menu bar.

 **Assessments**

Before you perform these exercises, restore the Assessment 3 portable company file from your file storage location and replace Mary's name with your own. If you need to review how to open a portable company file, see Hands-On 3.1.

Assessment 3.1   Manage the Vendor List

In this exercise, you will manage the Vendor List for Island Charters.

1. Using the following information, create three new Vendor List entries:

Name	Orlando's Bait Tank	Maury Electric Co.	Islanders Insurance
Address	3902 Old Beach Rd. Maury, WA 98069	3802 Maury Hwy. Maury, WA 98069	34679 SW 89th Maury, WA 98069
Phone	206-555-5465	206-555-3497	206-555-1116
Fax	None	206-555-3496	206-555-1117
Contact Name	Mr. Orlando Melvin	Ms. Amy McDonald	Mrs. Sharon Jones
Type	Supplies	Utilities	Insurance
Terms	Due on receipt	Net 30	Net 15
Account Number	IC79	4976-985	777698-4

2. Create a Vendor Contact List report and print it for your instructor.

Assessment 3.2   Perform Vendor Transactions

In this exercise, you will deal with expenses incurred by Island Charters.

Enter and Pay Bills

1. Enter a bill received on 5/03/2010 from Islanders Insurance for $598.

2. On 5/08/2010, Mary O'Malley received a bill from Orlando's Bait Tank for $59. Pass this expense on to YMCA Adventures. (Hint: Add **Bait** as a subaccount for Charter Expense.)

3. Enter a bill received on 5/9/2010 from Maury Electric Company for $100.94.

4. On 5/10/2010, Mary decided to sit down and pay her bills. Pay all of the bills that are due on or before 5/20/10.

5. Choose Done in the Payment Summary window.

Write and Print Checks

6. Mary took all of her employees out for a working lunch at Laura's Café on 5/15/2010. The total cost was $47.27. Enter this transaction, using check number 2113.

7. Create a check on 5/12/10 for $25.99, to be printed, made payable to Island Ford Service for auto service.

8. Print all of the checks waiting in the queue to be printed.

9. Run a Vendor Balance Detail report with the proper date range of May 2010 and print it for your instructor.

Assessment 3.3   Create Vendor Reports and Graphs

In this exercise, you will answer questions about Mary's business—Island Charters—by running the appropriate reports. You will continue to use the same file you used in Assessment 3.2.

1. Mary has asked for a report on how much she owes all vendors.

2. Now that her expenses and income have been entered into QuickBooks, Mary wants you to create a Profit & Loss report for her.

3. Create a graph that will show the Accounts Payable balances through 5/09/10.

4. QuickZoom in to determine where the balance for El Cajon Fill & Topsoil originated.

5. Print all of the reports and graphs you have created for your instructor.

6. Choose the appropriate option for your situation:
   - If you are continuing on to Lesson 4 or to the Critical Thinking exercises, leave Quick-Books open.
   - If you are finished working in QuickBooks, Choose File→Exit from the menu bar.

Critical Thinking

Critical Thinking 3.1 Work with Subcontractors

Griffin Construction has decided to take on subcontractors to do the electrical, plumbing, and drywall jobs. The owner has asked you to determine how to set up the subcontractors and keep them differentiated from the other vendors. When a customer is billed for a subcontractor's services, the owner wants to charge a higher price than he pays the subcontractor.

In a word processing document saved as **Critical Thinking 3.1**, describe how you would deal with this issue in QuickBooks. Submit the document to your instructor for evaluation.

Critical Thinking 3.2 Sort Through the Stack

The owner of Griffin Construction has hired you to help him catch up on his accounts payable transactions. Open the Critical Thinking 3 portable company file from your file storage location (you may already have it open from the last exercise). Enter the following vendor and payable transactions, using your best judgment as to how to deal with them:

- A bill dated 5/3/10 from Joan Walters Plumbing for $739.04 for subcontracted work

- A duplicate copy of check #1000 written on 5/9/10 to Minch's Catering for $278.35 for the food for the open house

- A sticky note stating that the work done by Hakkman's Plumbing on May 5 should be passed on to Ginger Howell and that an invoice should be created for her

- A bill from Sunland Electric Company dated 5/10/10 for $114.39 for electric service to the office

- A sticky note reading, "Print a check for House Depot for $200 for a down payment on a door being ordered for Susan Malimali—pass expense on to customer. Will stop by tomorrow (5/10/10) to drop it off."

- On 5/11/10, pay all bills that are outstanding or due

LESSON 4

Banking with QuickBooks

Before learning how to create a new company you should learn how to perform banking tasks in QuickBooks. With the advances in the Internet, online banking has become very commonplace. In this lesson, you will learn how to use QuickBooks banking features offline and the basics of working with QuickBooks online.

LESSON OBJECTIVES

After studying this lesson, you will be able to:

- Create bank accounts
- Transfer funds
- Manage credit card transactions
- Reconcile accounts
- Perform banking transactions online
- Work with banking reports

Integrative Case Study: Skortis Landscaping

Justin has been getting comfortable performing the basic vendor and customer transactions in QuickBooks. Justin's wife, Kathleen, is now going to take over the books because Justin has gotten quite busy with his customers. She will track banking transactions, work with the company's Chart of Accounts, deal with credit card transactions, and reconcile both the bank and credit card accounts.

Kathleen is interested in learning a little more about working with QuickBooks online as well.

Skortis Landscaping
Reconciliation Detail
Checking, Period Ending 05/17/2010

Type	Date	Num	Name	Clr	Amount	Balance
Beginning Balance						0.00
Cleared Transactions						
Checks and Payments - 8 items						
Check	4/27/2010	998	Steiger's Property M...	X	-1,000.00	-1,000.00
Check	4/27/2010	997	El Cajon Fill & Topsoil	X	-78.43	-1,078.43
Check	4/28/2010	999	The Corner Store	X	-42.13	-1,120.56
Check	4/28/2010	1000	Walley's Hardware	X	-7.64	-1,128.20
Bill Pmt -Check	5/10/2010	3000	Midland Telephone ...	X	-164.78	-1,292.98
Bill Pmt -Check	5/13/2010	3001	El Cajon Fill & Topsoil	X	-150.00	-1,442.98
Check	5/16/2010	1001	Chaparral Office Su...	X	-146.98	-1,589.96
Check	5/17/2010			X	-8.50	-1,598.46
Total Checks and Payments					-1,598.46	-1,598.46
Deposits and Credits - 4 items						
General Journal	4/26/2010	1		X	2,500.00	2,500.00
Deposit	5/8/2010			X	1,385.00	3,885.00
Deposit	5/14/2010			X	400.00	4,285.00
Transfer	5/15/2010			X	2,000.00	6,285.00
Total Deposits and Credits					6,285.00	6,285.00
Total Cleared Transactions					4,686.54	4,686.54
Cleared Balance					4,686.54	4,686.54
Uncleared Transactions						
Checks and Payments - 1 item						
Check	5/12/2010		Palomar Plant Supply		-587.00	-587.00
Total Checks and Payments					-587.00	-587.00
Total Uncleared Transactions					-587.00	-587.00
Register Balance as of 05/17/2010					4,099.54	4,099.54
Ending Balance					4,099.54	4,099.54

A Reconciliation Detail report displays all transactions that have cleared during the statement period and shows that the bank's and QuickBooks' balances match.

Creating Bank Accounts

The accounts you will work with in this lesson are assets (bank accounts) and liabilities (credit cards). There are two types of bank accounts you will deal with: Checking and Savings. Petty cash accounts will be covered in *QuickBooks Pro 2010: Level 2*.

Accessing Banking Activities in QuickBooks

The banking area on the Home page displays task icons for many of the activities you will perform in this lesson. The rest of the activities can be accessed via the menu bar.

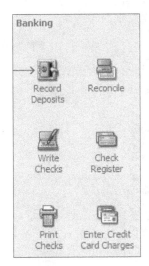

You can begin the reconciliation process by either clicking the task icon in the Banking area of the Home page or by choosing an option from the menu bar. To transfer funds and perform online banking activities you must use the menu bar.

The Chart of Accounts

The Chart of Accounts is composed of all of the asset, liability, equity, income, and expense accounts your company utilizes. You use the Chart of Accounts list window to create new accounts, edit existing accounts, and delete unused accounts. QuickBooks responds differently when you double-click items in the Chart of Accounts, depending on the type of account, as explained in the following table.

When you double-click this type of account...	QuickBooks responds by...
Any balance sheet account (asset, liability, or equity)	Opening an account register for that account. (Exception: The Retained Earnings account, which is a specially created account without a register. You will get a QuickReport when you double-click this account.)
Any income or expense account	Creating an account QuickReport.

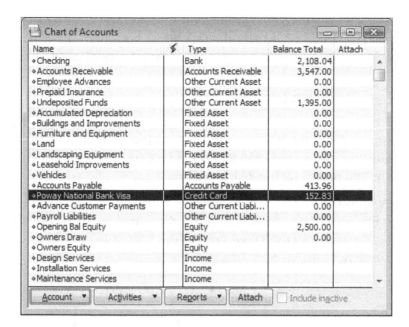

The Chart of Accounts window displays all accounts for a company. Notice that QuickBooks displays a balance for all balance sheet accounts (assets, liabilities, and equity), but not for income and expense accounts. The accounts are listed alphabetically *by type* (unless you have manually rearranged them). The highlighted account (in this case, Poway National Bank Visa) is the selected account, which will be affected if you issue a command using the menu buttons at the bottom of the window.

Editing an Existing Account

In order to edit an existing account in the Chart of Accounts, you need to first open it for editing. In the Edit Account window you will make changes similar to how you made them in Lesson 2, Working with Customer Transactions when editing a customer record. You will use the same editing techniques used in a word processing program to edit account information.

Creating a New Account

You will see the following window when you choose to create a new account in QuickBooks.

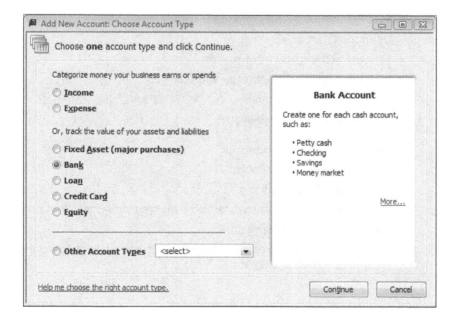

The Add New Account window will help to ensure that you choose the correct type of account when creating a new one.

In this lesson, we will be working with bank and credit card accounts. Notice the different types of accounts available in QuickBooks and the link at the bottom of the window, which will launch a Help window to assist you in choosing the correct type of account to create.

Working with an Account Register

Each balance sheet account (except for Retained Earnings) has its own register, which is a record of all transactions pertaining to the account. A QuickBooks register looks like the check register you may already keep for your personal checking account. The running balance automatically recalculates as you record each new transaction.

When you double-click within a transaction in a register, QuickBooks takes you to the source of the transaction. For instance, if you double-click the check transaction for Chaparral Office Supply in the following illustration, QuickBooks opens the Write Checks window with all information for the transaction displayed.

Date	Number	Payee		Payment	✓	Deposit	Balance
	Type	Account	Memo				
05/10/2010	3000	Midland Telephone Company		164.78			2,592.02
	BILLPMT	Accounts Payable	PW-74658-72				
05/12/2010	To Print	Palomar Plant Supply		587.00			2,005.02
	CHK	-split-	309VT				
05/13/2010	3001	El Cajon Fill & Topsoil		150.00			1,855.02
	BILLPMT	Accounts Payable	58-796				
05/14/2010						400.00	2,255.02
	DEP	Design Services	Deposit				

Notice that each transaction in the register includes two lines. The header at the top consists of two lines and describes what is found in each field.

QUICK REFERENCE: WORKING WITH THE CHART OF ACCOUNTS

Task	Procedure
Edit an account	■ Open the Chart of Accounts.
	■ Click the account you want to edit.
	■ Click the Account menu button and select Edit.
	■ Make any necessary changes.
	■ Click OK to accept the change(s).
Create a new account	■ Open the Chart of Accounts.
	■ Click the Account menu button.
	■ Choose New from the menu.
	■ Make sure you choose the correct account type, and then click Continue.
	■ Enter all necessary information.
	■ Click Save & Close to accept the new account, or click Save & New if you have additional accounts to create.

QUICK REFERENCE: WORKING WITH THE CHART OF ACCOUNTS (CONTINUED)

Task	Procedure
Delete an account	■ Open the Chart of Accounts.
	■ Click the account you want to delete.
	■ Click the Account menu button.
	■ Choose Delete from the menu.
	■ Click OK to confirm the deletion.
Open an account register	■ Open the Chart of Accounts.
	■ Double-click the balance sheet account for the register you wish to view.

 Hands-On 4.1   Work with the Chart of Accounts

In this exercise, you will open a portable company file and work with your Chart of Accounts.

Open a Portable Company File

The first steps are to open QuickBooks and to open the portable company file to use in this lesson.

1. Launch QuickBooks.

2. Choose File→Open or Restore Company from the menu bar.

3. Open the Hands-On Lesson 4 QuickBooks portable company file in your default storage location, placing your name as the first word in the filename (e.g., Justin Hands-On Lesson 4).

4. Click Remind Me Later in the Intuit Account window, if necessary.

Edit an Existing Account

There are several ways to open the Chart of Accounts; in this lesson you will use the task icon on the Home page.

Chart of Accounts

5. Click the Chart of Accounts task icon in the Company area of the Home page.

6. Scroll down, if necessary, and single-click the Poway National Bank Visa entry on the list.

7. Follow these steps to edit the account:

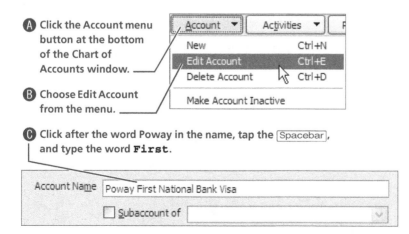

Ⓐ Click the Account menu button at the bottom of the Chart of Accounts window.

Ⓑ Choose Edit Account from the menu.

Ⓒ Click after the word Poway in the name, tap the [Spacebar], and type the word **First**.

Account Name | Poway First National Bank Visa

☐ Subaccount of

8. Click Save & Close to accept the account name change.

Create a New Account

9. Click the Account menu button at the bottom of the Chart of Accounts window and choose New.

10. Follow these steps to create a new bank account:

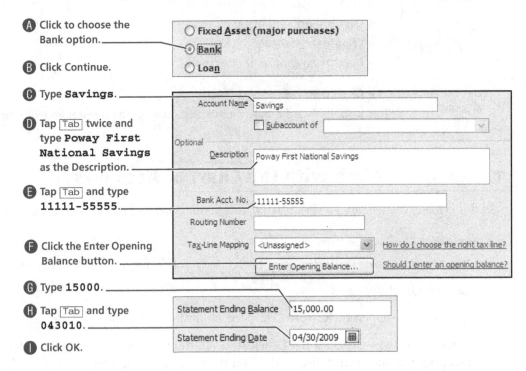

A Click to choose the Bank option.

B Click Continue.

C Type **Savings**.

D Tap [Tab] twice and type **Poway First National Savings** as the Description.

E Tap [Tab] and type **11111-55555**.

F Click the Enter Opening Balance button.

G Type **15000**.

H Tap [Tab] and type **043010**.

I Click OK.

You will need to talk to your tax advisor or accountant to determine which tax line your business should use.

11. Click Save & Close to record the new account, and then click No in the Set Up Online Services window.

QuickBooks will display the new bank account in the Chart of Accounts window.

Open and View a Register

12. Scroll up and double-click Checking in the Chart of Accounts window.

QuickBooks opens the Checking register. Take a moment to scroll up and view the transactions to date. You can also enter checks directly into the checking register rather than in the Write Checks window.

13. Follow these steps to view the original form of a bill payment:

Ⓐ Scroll up until you can see the 5/13/2010 transaction for El Cajon Fill & Topsoil.

Date	Number	Payee		Payment	✓	Deposit	Balance
	Type	Account	Memo				
05/12/2010	To Print	Palomar Plant Supply		587.00			2,005.02
	CHK	-split-	309VT				
05/13/2010	3001	El Cajon Fill & Topsoil		150.00			1,855.02
	BILLPMT	Accounts Payable	58 796				
05/14/2010						400.00	2,255.02
	DEP	Design Services	Deposit				
05/16/2010	1001	Chaparral Office Supply		146.98			2,108.04
	CHK	Office Supplies	Toner and printer i				

Ⓑ Double-click anywhere within the two lines of the transaction.

QuickBooks will take you to the Bill Payments (Check) - Checking window.

14. Choose Window→Close All from the menu bar.

Transferring Funds

Most people have transferred money between their bank accounts. QuickBooks has a feature that allows you to record this transfer. If you use online banking, you can even set QuickBooks to perform the transfer for you when you go online.

Since you are transferring funds between two asset accounts, you want to debit the account that is increasing and credit the account that is decreasing. Look at the following T-accounts to visualize this transaction.

BEHIND THE SCENES

In this illustration, you are transferring funds from the Savings account into the Checking account:

Checking	Savings
2,000	2,000

QUICK REFERENCE: TRANSFERRING FUNDS BETWEEN ACCOUNTS

Task	Procedure
Transfer funds	■ Choose Banking→Transfer Funds from the menu bar.
	■ Choose the account from which you want to draw the funds.
	■ Choose the account to which you want to send the funds.
	■ Type the amount to be transferred.
	■ Type a memo if you wish.
	■ Click Save & Close to record the transfer.

 Hands-On 4.2   Transfer Funds Between Accounts

In this exercise, Kathleen will transfer funds between the Checking and Savings accounts.

1. Choose Banking→Transfer Funds from the menu bar.

2. Follow these steps to complete the funds transfer:

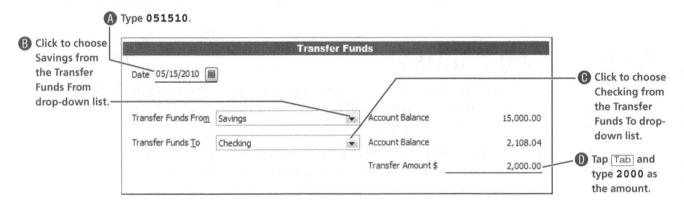

A Type **051510**.

B Click to choose Savings from the Transfer Funds From drop-down list.

C Click to choose Checking from the Transfer Funds To drop-down list.

D Tap Tab and type **2000** as the amount.

Notice that QuickBooks displays the account balances of the accounts involved in the transfer so you can verify sufficient funds are available.

3. Click Save & Close to record the transaction.

Managing Credit Card Transactions

Credit cards give business owners an easy way to track their expenses. QuickBooks allows you to track credit card transactions just as you track checking and savings account transactions. You can set up as many credit card accounts as you need; then, simply choose the account you want to work with in the Enter Credit Card Charges window.

If you use your personal credit cards occasionally for business purposes, you should not enter them in QuickBooks as business credit cards. Only create accounts for business credit cards.

Credit card transactions are classified as either a charge (when you make a purchase) or a credit (when you make a return). As you will use the same form for both types, you need to choose the correct type when entering transactions.

This drop-down arrow allows you to choose from all of your credit cards.

This drop-down arrow allows you to access your vendor list.

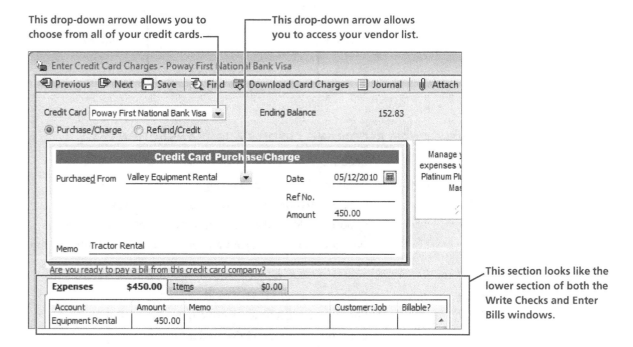

This section looks like the lower section of both the Write Checks and Enter Bills windows.

Type of Account and Normal Balance

A credit card is a liability, so its normal balance is a credit. This means you credit the account when you make a purchase (a "charge") and you debit the account when you make a payment (a "credit").

!TIP! *The term credit is a bit confusing at this point, as you will debit your credit card account if you enter a "credit" transaction. However, if you think of it from the perspective of the merchant, it makes perfect sense!*

BEHIND THE SCENES

A purchase credits the credit card account:

Poway FNB Visa		Office Supplies	
	78.96	78.96	

A payment debits the credit card account:

Poway FNB Visa		Checking	
152.83			152.83

QUICK REFERENCE: RECORDING CREDIT CARD TRANSACTIONS

Task	Procedure
Create a credit card account	■ Open the Chart of Accounts. ■ Click the Account menu button and choose New. ■ Choose Credit Card as the account type and click Continue. ■ Type the name of the card and any other relevant information. ■ Click OK.
Record a credit card transaction	■ Choose Banking→Enter Credit Card Charges. ■ Choose the account to record a purchase/refund to. ■ Enter the transaction information. ■ Click Save & Close to record the purchase/refund.

 Hands-On 4.3   Manage Credit Card Transactions

In this exercise, you will make a purchase with a credit card.

Record a Credit Card Purchase

Justin needs to rent a tractor for a job. The expense for the rental is $300; there is a refundable deposit of $150. You will enter transactions for both the rental and the safe return of the tractor.

1. Click the Home button on the icon bar.

2. Click the Enter Credit Card Charges task icon in the Banking area of the Home page.

3. Follow these steps to record the credit card charge:

(A) Tap [Tab] three times and type **Valley Equipment Rental** in the Purchased From field. Tap [Tab], click the Quick Add button, and click OK to set up Valley Equipment Rental as a new vendor.

(B) Type **051210**.

(C) Tap [Tab] twice and type **450** as the amount ($300 is the rental fee and $150 is a refundable deposit).

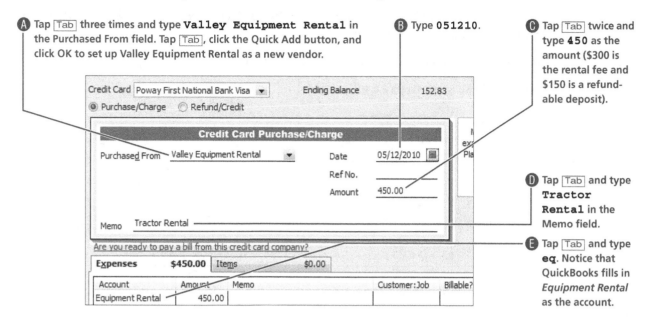

(D) Tap [Tab] and type **Tractor Rental** in the Memo field.

(E) Tap [Tab] and type **eq**. Notice that QuickBooks fills in *Equipment Rental* as the account.

4. Click the Save & New button.

Record a Credit Card Return

In the next transaction, Justin returns the tractor, and the rental company refunds the $150 deposit.

5. Follow these steps to complete the refund to your credit card:

(A) Click to choose the Refund/ Credit option.

(B) Tap [Tab] and type **v** to choose Valley Equipment Rental.

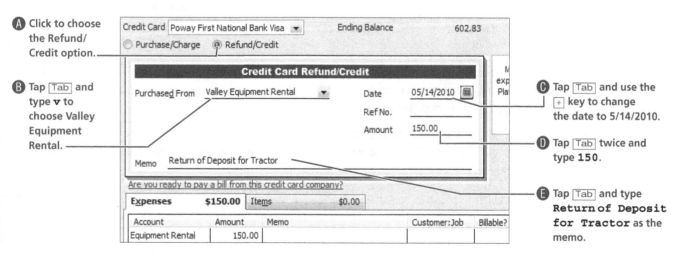

(C) Tap [Tab] and use the [+] key to change the date to 5/14/2010.

(D) Tap [Tab] twice and type **150**.

(E) Tap [Tab] and type **Return of Deposit for Tractor** as the memo.

Notice that QuickBooks will automatically fill in Equipment Rental *as the Account because you used it the last time you selected this vendor. You can either leave it as is or change it if a different account is affected this time. Because you used Poway FNB Visa in the last transaction, it will automatically fill into this form. You should also change the credit card account if you need to.*

6. Click the Save & Close button.
QuickBooks records your transaction and closes the transaction window.

Pay a Bill with a Credit Card

You can record a bill paid by credit card in QuickBooks, although you must use the Pay Bills window in order to properly affect Accounts Payable.

7. Click the Pay Bills task icon in the Vendors area of the Home page.

8. Follow these steps to pay a bill with a credit card:

Ⓐ Click to place a checkmark in the box for El Cajon Fill & Topsoil.

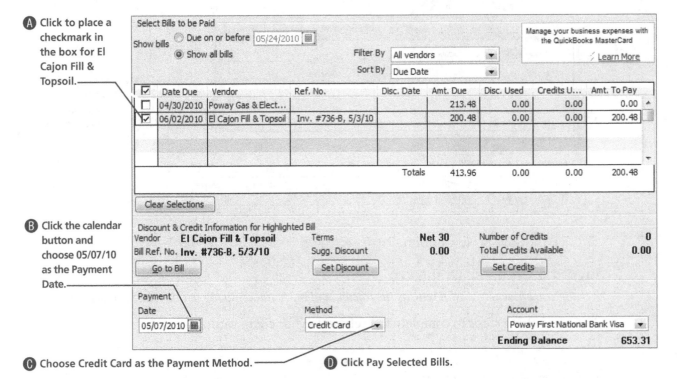

Ⓑ Click the calendar button and choose 05/07/10 as the Payment Date.

Ⓒ Choose Credit Card as the Payment Method.

Ⓓ Click Pay Selected Bills.

Notice that when you choose Credit Card as the method of payment, Poway First National Bank Visa automatically fills in as the Payment Account. If you have multiple credit card accounts, make sure that the correct account is displayed in the Payment Account section of the window.

9. Click Done in the Payment Summary window.
QuickBooks will record the bill payment in both the Accounts Payable and the Poway First National Bank Visa registers.

Reconciling Accounts

It is important to make sure that your account records in QuickBooks match those of the bank. The process of matching your accounts to the bank statements you receive is called reconciliation.

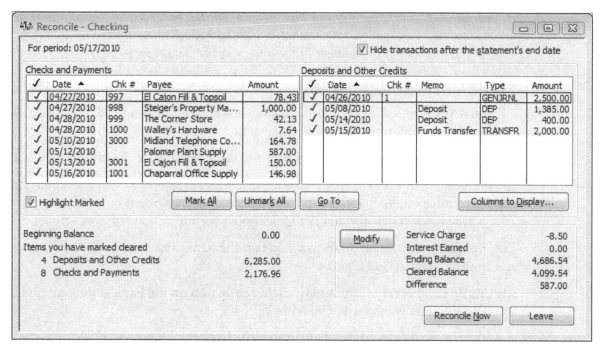

QuickBooks bank account reconciliation window.

QuickBooks' Reconciliation Features

You should be aware of some important reconciliation features in QuickBooks. You can save your reconciliation reports in PDF (Portable Document Format) so that they are ready to send via email and are viewable with the free Adobe Reader program (also known as Acrobat Reader). In QuickBooks Pro, when you reconcile a new statement the reconciliation report replaces the prior report with the new month's information. You should save each report in PDF to a storage location such as your hard drive or a network drive if you are using the Pro edition. In QuickBooks Premier and Enterprise editions, QuickBooks saves all of the reconciliation reports as PDF files for you and you can access them through QuickBooks at any time.

Locating Discrepancies

QuickBooks also provides a feature that helps you locate discrepancies if there is a difference in balances during the reconciliation process. You can run a Reconciliation Discrepancy Report that lists transactions affecting the reconciliation balance. The types of transactions that can affect the balance are:

- Deleted transactions

- A change to a previously cleared amount

- Transactions that were manually uncleared in the register

- Transactions in which the date was changed to a different statement period

When Your Accounts Don't Match

It is important to take the time when performing reconciliations to ensure there are no errors. As you clear each transaction, make sure the amounts are exactly the same. It is very frustrating when you get to the end of the transactions and don't balance.

 TIP! *Once you have cleared transactions through the reconciliation process, it is important to **not** change them. Changes may alter your starting balance for the next reconciliation. If you find yourself in such a situation, you can run a Reconciliation Discrepancy report to find the problem(s).*

Problem Resolution Process

If you do find yourself in the unfavorable situation of finishing your reconciliation without balancing, consider the following suggestions:

- Look for a transaction that is exactly the same amount as the difference and ensure whether or not it should be cleared.

- Determine whether you are missing a deposit or a payment by looking at the totals of each on the bank statement and the QuickBooks reconciliation window.

- Compare the number of transactions on the bank statement to the number of cleared transactions in QuickBooks.

- Verify the individual amount of each transaction on the bank statement and compare it to the amounts you have in QuickBooks.

- Determine whether it is a bank error (the bank may have recorded a transaction for the wrong amount).

- If it is a bank error, you can have QuickBooks create an adjustment transaction, notify the bank, and then reverse the adjustment transaction after the bank corrects the error.

- Run a Reconciliation Discrepancy report to see if any changes were made to previously cleared transactions.

- If changes were made to previously cleared transactions, undo the last reconciliation and redo it.

Reconciling Credit Cards

You can reconcile your credit cards the same way as you reconcile your bank account.

Once you have reconciled the credit card, you have the option to pay any amount due. You can choose to either write a check or enter a bill for the payment. QuickBooks takes the balance due on the credit card and fills it in to either the Enter Bills or the Write Checks window. If you don't plan to pay the entire bill, you can change the amount manually.

QR

QUICK REFERENCE: PERFORMING ACCOUNT RECONCILIATION

Task	Procedure
Reconcile a bank account	■ Choose Banking→Reconcile from the menu bar.
	■ Choose the account and enter the date of the bank statement and ending balance.
	■ Enter any finance charges.
	■ Click Continue.
	■ Choose to show transactions on or before the statement ending date only.
	■ Compare the QuickBooks transactions to the bank statement and mark off all cleared transactions.
	■ When the difference is zero, click the Reconcile Now button.
Reconcile a credit card	■ Open the Chart of Accounts.
	■ Single-click on the account you wish to reconcile.
	■ Click the Activities button at the bottom of the window and choose Reconcile Credit Card.
	■ Choose the account and enter the date of the credit card statement and ending balance.
	■ Enter any finance charges.
	■ Click Continue.
	■ Choose to show transactions on or before the statement ending date only.
	■ Compare the QuickBooks transactions to the credit card statement and mark off all cleared transactions.
	■ When the difference is zero, click the Reconcile Now button.

In this exercise, you will use the QuickBooks reconciliation features for both a bank account and a credit card account.

Before you begin: You will be working with a bank statement and a credit card statement in this exercise. You can use the illustrations of the statements provided in the book, or you can print them from your file storage location. The files available for printing are Hands-On 4.4 Checking Statement and Hands-On 4.4 Credit Card Statement.

Prepare to Reconcile a Checking Account

First, you will prepare to help Kathleen reconcile the checking account for Skortis Landscaping. The bank statement for this account that you will use to complete the reconciliation is displayed here.

Poway First National Bank
487 Merrifield Avenue
Poway, CA 92064

Statement of Account Prepared For:
  Skortis Landscaping
  876 Lauri Street
  Poway, CA 92064

                              Account Number: 11111-44444

                      Statement Period: April 18 - May 17, 2010

Total Deposits:	$6,285.00	Total Payments:	$1,773.46
Beginning Balance:	$0.00	Ending Balance:	$4,511.54

Transactions:

Date	Transaction type	Payment	Deposit	Balance
	Beginning Balance			$0.00
4/26/2010	Deposit		2,500.00	2,500.00
4/27/2010	Check #997	78.43		2,421.57
4/27/2010	Check #998	1,000.00		1,421.57
4/28/2010	Check #999	42.13		1,379.44
4/28/2010	Check #1000	7.64		1,371.80
5/8/2010	Deposit		1,385.00	2,756.80
5/10/2010	Check #3000	164.78		2,592.02
5/13/2010	Check #3001	150.00		2,442.02
5/14/2010	Deposit		400.00	2,842.02
5/15/2010	Transfer from Savings		2,000.00	4,842.02
5/16/2010	Check #1001	146.98		4,695.04
5/17/2010	Service Charge	8.50		4,686.54
	Ending Balance			4,686.54

---

1. Click the Reconcile task icon in the Banking area of the Home page.
   QuickBooks displays the Begin Reconciliation window. If the Home page is not visible, choose Company→Home Page from the menu bar.

2. Using the figure provided or the bank statement you printed, follow these steps to prepare for reconciliation:

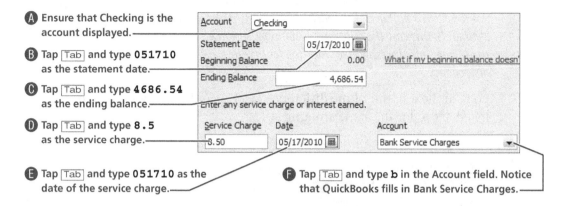

A Ensure that Checking is the account displayed.

B Tap [Tab] and type **051710** as the statement date.

C Tap [Tab] and type **4686.54** as the ending balance.

D Tap [Tab] and type **8.5** as the service charge.

E Tap [Tab] and type **051710** as the date of the service charge.

F Tap [Tab] and type **b** in the Account field. Notice that QuickBooks fills in Bank Service Charges.

3. Tap [Tab], and then click Continue to move on to the Reconcile-Checking window.
   The Reconcile-Checking window shows all transactions waiting to be cleared.

Reconcile a Checking Account

Now that you have completed the Begin Reconciliation window, you are ready to begin the actual reconciliation.

4. Click in the "Hide transactions after the statement's ending date" box.
   Notice that check number 101 and the deposit dated 5/14/10 are no longer visible in the window. This feature makes it a lot easier to find the transactions you need to clear without having to sort through the more recent ones (this is especially helpful if you are playing catch-up with your reconciling!).

5. Click the Mark All button to place a checkmark in front of each transaction.
   You eliminated the transactions that occurred after the statement ending date and all of the remaining transactions are shown on the bank statement. If any of the transactions were not on the bank statement, you could click the checkmark to the left of them to remove them as cleared items.

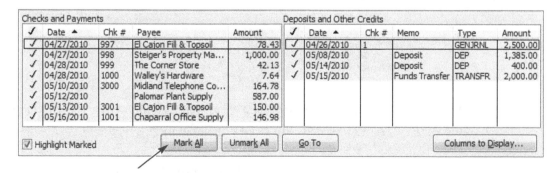

6. Look at the Difference line to see if it is zero.
   When reconciling, your goal is to show a difference of zero between your QuickBooks cleared balance and the bank's cleared balance after marking all of the items cleared. In this case the difference is not zero, so you will need to do some investigative work to identify the discrepancy.

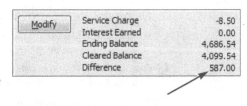

7. Look at the amount of the difference ($587), and then look to see if there is a transaction listed above for the same amount.

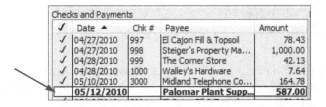

   The first step in the Problem Resolution Process section on page 122 is to look for a transaction that is exactly the same amount as the difference and determine whether it should be cleared. Notice that there is a transaction for $587. This is the check that you chose not to print in the previous lesson, so it should not be marked as cleared.

8. Click once to remove the checkmark to the left of the 5/12/2010 transaction for Palomar Plant Supply.

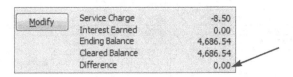

9. Look again at the Difference line to ensure that it is now zero.

Modify	Service Charge	-8.50
	Interest Earned	0.00
	Ending Balance	4,686.54
	Cleared Balance	4,686.54
	Difference	0.00

   You just performed some basic "sleuthing" to get your account to reconcile. In many cases, it will take more steps to find the problem. Just be persistent and work through the list provided, and you will become a pro at reconciling accounts!

10. Click the Reconcile Now button. Click OK in the Information window, if necessary.
    There is a pause as QuickBooks records the marked transactions as cleared. Pat yourself on the back as QuickBooks has just congratulated you on a successful reconciliation.

11. Click the Close button to choose to not produce a report at this time.
    You will learn about reconciliation reports later in this lesson.

Prepare to Reconcile a Credit Card Account

The process of reconciling a credit card account is quite similar to the process you just used to reconcile a bank statement. You can either use the illustration provided or the one you may have printed before starting this exercise.

Poway First National Bank
487 Merrifield Avenue
Poway, CA 92064

Visa Statement Prepared For:
Skortis Landscaping
876 Lauri Street
Poway, CA 92064

Account Number: 4444 2222 4444 2222

Statement Period: April 16 - May 15, 2010

Total Charges:	$452.83	Total Payments:	$0.00
Beginning Balance:	$0.00	Ending Balance:	$452.83

Transactions:

Date	Description	Charge	Credit	Balance
	Beginning Balance			$0.00
5/6/2010	Chapparral Office Supply	75.86		$75.86
5/9/2010	The Corner Store	33.46		$109.32
5/12/2010	Walley's Hardware	43.51		$152.83
5/12/2010	Valley Equipment Rental	450.00		$602.83
5/14/2010	Valley Equipment Rental		150.00	$452.83
5/15/2010	Periodic Finance Charge	0		$452.83
	Ending Balance			$452.83

12. Choose Lists→Chart of Accounts from the menu bar.

13. Scroll down, if necessary, and single-click to choose Poway First National Bank Visa from the list.

14. Click the Activities button at the bottom of the Chart of Accounts window and choose Reconcile Credit Card from the menu.

15. Using the credit card statement you just printed or the figure provided, follow these steps to prepare for reconciliation:

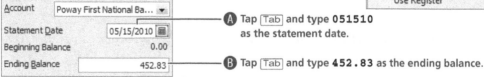

Ⓐ Tap ⟨Tab⟩ and type **051510** as the statement date.

Ⓑ Tap ⟨Tab⟩ and type **452.83** as the ending balance.

16. Click Continue to begin reconciling.

Reconcile the Credit Card Account

17. Follow these steps to complete the reconciliation:

Ⓐ Look at the credit card statement and click to the left of each of the charges/cash advances that appear on the statement; a checkmark will appear with each click.

Ⓑ Look at the credit card statement and click to the left of each of the payments/credits that appear on the statement; a checkmark will appear with each click.

Charges and Cash Advances					Payments and Credits					
✓	Date ▲	Ref #	Payee	Amount	✓	Date ▲	Ref #	Memo	Type	Amo...
✓	05/06/2010		Chaparral Office Supply	75.86	✓	05/14/2010		Return of Depo...	CC CRED	150.00
✓	05/09/2010		The Corner Store	33.46						
✓	05/12/2010		Walley's Hardware	43.51						
✓	05/12/2010		Valley Equipment Rental	450.00						
	05/17/2010		El Cajon Fill & Topsoil	200.48						

☑ Highlight Marked   [Mark All] [Unmark All] [Go To]   [Columns to Display...]

Beginning Balance	0.00		[Modify]	Finance Charge	0.00
Items you have marked cleared				Ending Balance	452.83
1 Payments and Credits	150.00			Cleared Balance	452.83
4 Charges and Cash Advances	602.83			Difference	0.00

Ⓒ Look at the Difference number to see if it is zero, which is your goal. ─────

If you do not have a difference of zero, look back at the Problem Resolution Process section on page 122 for troubleshooting ideas as to how to resolve the difference. Note that you could have clicked the Mark All button, as you did when you reconciled the bank account, and then clicked to the left of the El Cajon Fill & Topsoil transaction to unmark it. You can use either method in each of the reconciliation windows.

18. Click the Reconcile Now button to clear all marked transactions in your QuickBooks file.
Since you have a balance due on the credit card, QuickBooks opens a Make Payment window that allows you to make a payment on your credit card at the end of the reconciliation process. Leave this window open.

Enter a Bill for a Partial Payment on the Credit Card Account

You can either enter a bill for the payment amount or write a check. You will enter a bill in this exercise.

19. Choose the Enter a Bill for Payment Later option.

Payment
○ Write a check for payment now
◉ Enter a bill for payment later

20. Click OK to continue.
There is a pause as QuickBooks records the cleared transactions and opens the Enter Bills window. Once the transactions are cleared, QuickBooks displays a congratulatory message.

21. Click the Close button at the bottom of the Select Reconciliation Report window to bypass creating a report.
QuickBooks displays the Enter Bills window.

22. Follow these steps to complete the bill entry:

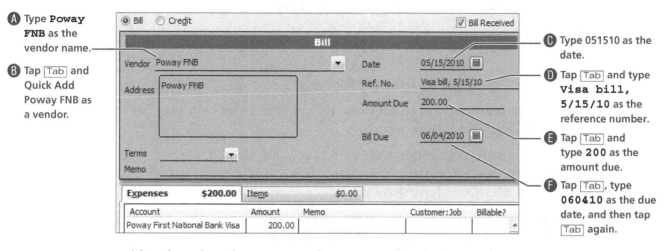

Ⓐ Type **Poway FNB** as the vendor name.

Ⓑ Tap Tab and Quick Add Poway FNB as a vendor.

Ⓒ Type 051510 as the date.

Ⓓ Tap Tab and type **Visa bill, 5/15/10** as the reference number.

Ⓔ Tap Tab and type **200** as the amount due.

Ⓕ Tap Tab, type **060410** as the due date, and then tap Tab again.

QuickBooks updates the amount on the Expenses tab at the bottom of the window. Notice that Quick-Books has already filled in the account that will be debited (Poway First National Visa).

23. Click Save & Close to record the bill and close the window.
QuickBooks returns to the Chart of Accounts window.

24. Close the Chart of Account window.

Viewing Banking Reports

The banking feature of QuickBooks comes with preset reports for you to use to get answers from your data. Banking reports deal with answers to questions such as:

- What are all of the transactions involving a specific payee?
- What checks have not cleared the bank as of the last bank statement?
- Which payments still need to be deposited?
- Where can I find a list of all transactions that affect my checking account?
- What changes in transactions may affect my next reconciliation?

Register QuickReports

Register QuickReports are run right from a register window. Once you have selected a transaction and clicked the QuickReport button, you will receive a report that shows all transactions for the payee of the selected transaction.

This is an example of a register Quick-Report based on Skortis Landscaping's transactions with El Cajon Fill & Topsoil.

Reconciliation Reports

Reconciliation reports show transactions that have cleared and that have yet to clear the bank. Beginning with the QuickBooks 2004 version, you can save reconciliation reports in PDF; in prior versions, you can only run a report for the last reconciliation performed.

Alternatives to Printing Reports

Of course you can send any report to the printer. QuickBooks also gives you additional options for storing or working with a report:

■ **Email**—QuickBooks can convert the report to PDF format, which can be viewed with the free Adobe Reader program. This allows viewing of the report exactly as it would print even to those who do not have QuickBooks.

■ **Export**—QuickBooks can export the report to Microsoft Excel so you can use Excel's powerful spreadsheet features to work with your data.

QUICK REFERENCE: CREATING BANKING REPORTS

Task	Procedure
Produce a register QuickReport	■ Open the register from which you wish to create the report. ■ Click within the transaction on which you want to base the report. ■ Click QuickReport on the register toolbar.
Produce a reconciliation report	■ Choose Reports→Banking→Previous Reconciliation from the menu bar. ■ Choose the correct account and the statement ending date. ■ Choose whether you want a detail or summary report (or both). ■ Click Display.
Produce a reconciliation discrepancy report	■ Choose Reports→Banking→Reconciliation Discrepancy from the menu bar. ■ Choose the correct account. ■ Click OK.

 Hands-On 4.5   Produce Banking-Related Reports

In this exercise, you will produce three banking reports for Skortis Landscaping: a register report, a deposit detail report, and a reconciliation report.

Run a Register QuickReport

This first report helps you determine exactly how much you have paid to a particular payee.

1. Choose Banking→Use Register from the menu bar.
   This button opens a window from which you can choose a register on which to base the report.

2. Click OK to choose the Checking account.
   QuickBooks displays the Checking register window.

3. Follow these steps to produce the register QuickReport:

Ⓐ Scroll up until you see one of the El Cajon Fill & Topsoil transactions.

Ⓑ Single-click anywhere within the two-line transaction.

Date	Number	Payee		Payment	✓	Deposit	Balance
	Type	Account	Memo				
05/12/2010	To Print	Palomar Plant Supply		587.00			2,005.02
	CHK	-split-	309VT				
05/13/2010	3001	El Cajon Fill & Topsoil		150.00	✓		1,855.02
	BILLPMT	Accounts Payable	58-796				
05/14/2010					✓	400.00	2,255.02
	DEP	Design Services	Deposit				

Toolbar: ⬍ Go to... | 🖨 Print... | 📝 Edit Transaction | 📋 QuickReport | 📄 Download Bank Statement

Ⓒ Click the QuickReport button on the toolbar of the register window.

Notice the various buttons you can use to print, email, export, and perform other tasks with this report.

4. Choose Window→Close All from the menu bar.

QuickBooks returns you to an empty QuickBooks Desktop.

Run a Deposit Detail Report

This report displays an accounting of all of the deposits for the date range you specify.

5. Choose Reports→Banking→Deposit Detail from the menu bar.

6. Type **a** to set the date range to All.

You will see a report detailing all of the deposit transactions.

7. Close the Deposit Detail report window, choosing to not memorize the report.

Run a Reconciliation Report

In this report, you will view the result of the reconciliation you performed earlier in this lesson.

8. Choose Reports→Banking→Previous Reconciliation from the menu bar.

9. If necessary, choose Checking from the Account field drop-down list.

Account	Type of Report
Checking ⌄	○ Summary
	⦿ Detail
	○ Both

10. Click the Display button to produce the report.

QuickBooks generates this report as a PDF file that can be saved, printed, and/or emailed. Anyone can view PDF files with the free Adobe Reader program available from Adobe Systems (http://adobe.com). To view a PDF copy of this report, visit the website for this course at labpub.com/learn/qb10_QC1/.

11. Close the Reconciliation Detail window.

12. Choose the appropriate option for your situation:

- If you are continuing on to Lesson 5 or to the end-of-lesson exercises, leave QuickBooks open and read the Going Online with QuickBooks section.
- If you are finished working in QuickBooks, Choose File→Exit from the menu bar.

Going Online with QuickBooks

There are a variety of tasks that can be carried out online with QuickBooks. You can manage your documents, bank online, and pay bills online to name a few. In Lesson 1, Introducing QuickBooks Pro, you learned about the Marketing Center and Customer Manager, both of which are also online tools designed to help you to work with QuickBooks more efficiently.

Managing Documents in QuickBooks

With the 2010 version, QuickBooks has made it easier than ever for you to keep track of all business documents in one place. The document management feature allows a QuickBooks user to attach electronic documentation to any transaction; or you can attach documents to a customer, vender, or employee account.

In order to take advantage of this service, you must first register with Intuit. You can save about 1,000 two-page documents (in a PDF format) for free, and if you need more space you can purchase a monthly subscription plan. The documents are stored online on the Intuit server, and you can choose to give secure access to your accountant or others who may need the information.

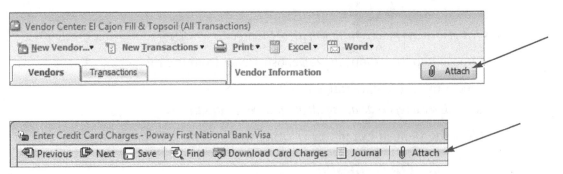

Notice the Attach buttons available in the Vendor Information area of the Vendor Center and at the top of the Enter Credit Card Charges window.

Online Banking Features

QuickBooks contains many online banking features. Some of the program's most useful online banking capabilities enable you to:

- **Access Accounts Online and Download Information**—QuickBooks allows you to download transactions and account information once you have set up your account(s) for online banking. You can use this feature to easily reconcile your account, too.

- **Transfer Funds Online**—If you have more than one account at the same financial institution, you can set up a transfer between accounts in QuickBooks. When you go online with QuickBooks, the transfer will be made for you.

- **Make Payments Online**—Some financial institutions allow you to pay bills online through QuickBooks. If your institution doesn't offer this service, Intuit has a service to which you can subscribe. To process a check as an online payment, you must set up the vendor by including his name, address, phone number, and account number by which he identifies you in the Vendor List.

There is even a new online banking setup wizard in QuickBooks 2010 that streamlines the process for you.

Preparing for Online Banking with QuickBooks

Before you can use the online banking features in QuickBooks, you must complete an application with your financial institution and receive a confirmation letter with a personal identification number (PIN) in the mail. Charges for this service vary by financial institution. Contact your financial institution to find out the charges and functionality with QuickBooks.

QUICK REFERENCE: GOING ONLINE WITH QUICKBOOKS

Task	Procedure
Set up an account for online access	■ Contact your financial institution and complete an application for QuickBooks online services.
	■ Choose Banking→Online Banking→Setup Account for Online Services.
	■ Progress through the steps in the Setup Account for Online Services interview.

 **Concepts Review**

True/False Questions

1. In QuickBooks, Credit Card is a type of bank account.   TRUE   FALSE

2. Only bank accounts have registers that detail all transactions for the account.   TRUE   FALSE

3. When you double-click a liability in the Chart of Accounts, a QuickReport will   TRUE   FALSE
   be displayed.

4. QuickBooks can perform an online funds transfer between your accounts at the   TRUE   FALSE
   same bank if you are set up for online banking.

5. Reconciliation is the process of matching your QuickBooks bank accounts to the   TRUE   FALSE
   statements you receive from the bank.

6. In QuickBooks Premiere, you can only run a report for the last reconciliation you   TRUE   FALSE
   performed.

7. The Chart of Accounts lists only your company's bank accounts.   TRUE   FALSE

8. A Reconciliation Discrepancy report helps you find the transactions changed since   TRUE   FALSE
   your last reconciliation.

9. Reconciliation reports only display transactions cleared by the bank.   TRUE   FALSE

10. If you have online banking set up, QuickBooks allows you to download your   TRUE   FALSE
    checking account transactions so you don't have to enter them by hand.

Multiple Choice Questions

1. Which of the following tasks can you *not* perform online with QuickBooks?

   a. Download transactions from your bank to your QuickBooks file

   b. Pay your bills

   c. Upload your transactions from your QuickBooks file to your bank

   d. Transfer money between accounts

2. What is the first thing to do if you cleared QuickBooks transactions and the bank statement doesn't balance after reconciling?

   a. Look for a transaction with the same amount as the difference.

   b. Click the Unmark All button so you can start over.

   c. Go through all of the deposit transactions and make sure they are checked.

   d. Go through all of the payment transactions and make sure they are the correct amounts.

3. When you pay your credit card bill with a check, what occurs behind the scenes?

   a. You debit the checking account and credit the credit card account.

   b. You debit both the checking and the credit card accounts.

   c. You credit the checking account and debit the credit card account.

   d. You credit both the checking and the credit card accounts.

4. What type of report should you run if you want to see all the transactions affecting one vendor for the current month?

   a. Profit & Loss

   b. Register

   c. Reconciliation

   d. Balance Sheet

Skill Builders

Before you begin these exercises, restore the Skill Builder 4 portable company file in QuickBooks from your file storage location, placing your name as the first word in the filename (e.g., Susie Skill Builder 4).

Skill Builder 4.1   Work with Bank Accounts

In this exercise, you will take care of the banking tasks for The Tea Shoppe.

Create a Money Market Account

Susie's business checking account earns no interest so she has decided to open a money market account at the same bank.

1. Choose Lists→Chart of Accounts from the menu bar.

2. Click the Account menu button and choose New from the menu.

3. Choose Bank as the account type and click Continue.

4. Type **Money Market** as the new account name.

5. Click Save & Close, choosing No in the Set Up Online Services window.

Make a Deposit

Susie did a cooking demonstration for a local organization. She needs to deposit the fee she earned into her checking account.

6. Choose Banking→Make Deposits from the menu bar.

7. Choose Checking as the Deposit To account. Click OK if the default account information window appears in order to acknowledge it and move to the Make Deposits window.

8. Enter the deposit on 5/20/10, using Catering Sales as the income account.
   Remember, you do not have to enter a customer, but you must enter an income account!

9. The payment is in the form of a check number **753** for **$800**.

10. Click Save & Close to record the transaction and close the window.

Transfer Funds Between Accounts

Since the money market account earns interest, Susie has decided to transfer some funds from her checking account into it.

11. Choose Banking→Transfer Funds from the menu bar.

12. Set the date to 5/23/10.

13. Choose Checking as the Transfer Funds From account.

14. Choose Money Market as the Transfer Funds To account.

15. Type **10000** as the transfer amount.

16. Click Save & Close to record the transfer and close the window.

Reconcile the Checking Account

The bank statement has just arrived so it is time to reconcile it to The Tea Shoppe's QuickBooks account. You may print your own statement (Skill Builder 4.1 Bank Statement) from your default storage location, or refer to the illustration shown after step 18.

17. Choose Banking→Reconcile from the menu bar.

18. Using the statement you printed or the following copy, reconcile the Checking account for Susie:

ROP Credit Union
487 Merrifield Avenue
Lake San Marcos, CA 92078

Statement of Account Prepared For:
The Tea Shoppe at the Lake
Susie Elsasser
316 Swan Drive
Lake San Marcos, CA 92078

Account Number: 555-777

Statement Period: April 24 - May 23, 2010

Total Deposits:	$5,960.71	Total Payments:	$11,990.86
Beginning Balance:	$23,000.00	Ending Balance:	$16,969.85

Transactions:

Date	Transaction type	Payment	Deposit	Balance
	Beginning Balance			$23,000.00
4/24/2010	Check #1894	75.49		$22,924.51
4/26/2010	Check #1895	1,200.00		21,724.51
4/27/2010	Check #1896	346.70		21,377.81
4/29/2010	Deposit		75.00	21,452.81
4/29/2010	Check #1897	68.43		21,384.38
4/29/2010	Check #1898	34.52		21,349.86
4/30/2010	Deposit		1,146.71	22,496.57
5/3/2010	Check #1899	135.72		22,360.85
5/6/2010	Check #1900	125.00		22,235.85
5/9/2010	Deposit		1,939.00	24,174.85
5/15/2010	Deposit		2,000.00	26,174.85
5/20/2010	Deposit		800.00	26,974.85
5/23/2010	Transfer to Savings	10,000.00		16,974.85
5/23/2010	Service Charge	5.00		16,969.85
	Ending Balance			16,969.85

Pay attention to the following hints when you reconcile:

■ *In the Begin Reconciliation window, make sure you enter the ending balance and the service charge.*

■ *In the Reconcile-Checking window, make sure to mark only those transactions that have cleared the bank (and are on the bank statement) and that have zero differences before you click Reconcile Now.*

■ *If the difference is not zero, see the Problem Resolution Process section on page 122.*

19. Choose to not create a reconciliation report now.

Skill Builder 4.2   Manage Credit Card Transactions

In this exercise, you will help Susie set up her new Visa credit card in QuickBooks.

Create a New Credit Card Account

1. If your Chart of Accounts window is not open, choose Lists→Chart of Accounts from the menu bar.

2. Click the Account menu button and choose New from the context menu.

3. Choose Credit Card as the account type, and then click Continue.

4. Name the new account **Kirkland Visa**.

5. Click Save & Close to enter the new account and close the window, choosing No when asked if you want to set up online services.

Enter a Credit Card Charge

Susie is purchasing new aprons for the business. She is not sure of the color for one of the aprons, so she will purchase two and later return one of them.

6. Choose Banking→Enter Credit Card Charges from the menu bar.

7. Tap [Tab] three times and type **Betty's Boutique** as the vendor. Tap [Tab] again and choose to Quick Add it as a vendor.

8. Set the date to 5/25/10, tap [Tab] twice, and type **$150** as the amount.

9. Click in the Account column and choose **Uniforms** as the expense account.

10. Click Save & New to record the transaction.

Enter a Credit Card Credit

Now you will process the uniform return for Susie. The Enter Credit Card Charges window should still be open from the last step; if it isn't, choose Banking→Record Credit Card Charges→Enter Credit Card Charges from the menu bar.

11. Choose Betty's Boutique as the vendor.

12. Set the date to 5/27/10.

13. Choose the Refund/Credit option to show it is a return.

14. Type **$30** as the amount and ensure that Uniforms is the account.

15. Click Save & Close to record the refund and close the window.

Skill Builder 4.3　Produce Banking Reports

Susie wants to run some banking reports to get answers from her data. In this exercise, you will help her do just that.

Produce a Reconciliation Report

Susie already performed a reconciliation; now you will produce the reconciliation report for her.

1. Choose Reports→Banking→Previous Reconciliation from the menu bar.

2. Click Display to produce the report.

3. Print the report and then close the Reconciliation Detail window.

Run a Deposit Detail Report

Susie would like to see all of her bank deposits for May, so she will run a report to display them.

4. Choose Reports→Banking→Deposit Detail from the menu bar.

5. Tap ⌜Tab⌟, type **050110**, and then tap ⌜Tab⌟ again and type **053110**.

6. Click the Refresh button on the report toolbar.
   You will see a report that displays the details for each deposit in May.

 TIP! *If you tap ⌜Tab⌟ after changing the date, QuickBooks will automatically refresh the report for you, too.*

7. Close the Deposit Details report window, clicking No when asked to memorize the report.

Create a Checking Account QuickReport

Susie wants to print a report showing all transactions in the Checking account from 5/7/10 to 5/27/10. Earlier in this lesson you produced a QuickReport from the register. Now you will produce an account QuickReport from the Chart of Accounts.

8. If your Chart of Accounts window is not open, choose Lists→Chart of Accounts from the menu bar.

9. Scroll up and single-click Checking to select the account.

10. Click the Reports button at the bottom of the Chart of Accounts window and choose QuickReport:Checking from the menu.

11. Tap ⌜Tab⌟ and type **050710** in the From (date) field; tap ⌜Tab⌟ again and type **052710** as the ending date.

12. Click the Refresh button on the report toolbar.
    QuickBooks will regenerate the report based on the changes you made.

13. Close the Account Quick Report.

14. Choose the appropriate option for your situation:
    - If you are continuing on to Lesson 5 or to the rest of the end-of-lesson exercises, leave QuickBooks open.
    - If you are finished working in QuickBooks, Choose File→Exit from the menu bar.

# Assessments

Before you perform any of these exercises, restore the Assessment 4 portable company file from your file storage location and place your name as the first word in the filename (e.g., Mary Assessment 4). Click Remind Me Later if the Intuit Account window appears.

Assessment 4.1   Manage Banking and Credit Card Transactions

Mary O'Malley has just opened a new savings account and received her new corporate American Express.

1. Open the Chart of Accounts and create two new accounts for Island Charters: **Savings** (bank account number 6526-7387) and **American Express** (credit card number 3999 888888 00000). Choose to not set up online services for either account.

2. Transfer $10,000 from the Checking account to the Savings account on 5/23/2010.

3. Enter the following American Express charges for the month:
   Quick Add any vendors not on the Vendor List, create a new expense account if necessary, and use your best judgment in selecting an expense account.

Date	Vendor	Amount	Memo
5/1/10	Thrifty Grocery	$26.73	Office coffee mess
5/4/10	Dock Fuel Service	$108.70	Fuel for boat
5/6/10	Malimali Hardware Store	$43.20	Supplies
5/8/10	The Boat Store	$94.85	Equipment for boat
5/11/10	Thrifty Grocery	$18.49	Birthday cake
5/14/10	Dock Fuel Service	$115.43	Fuel for boat
5/17/10	Sam's Service Station	$26.71	Fuel for company car
5/20/10	The Boat Store	($33.75) credit	Equipment for boat
5/28/10	Dock Fuel Service	$99.78	Fuel for boat

Assessment 4.2   Reconcile an Account

Mary has just received her American Express statement. In this exercise, you will help Mary reconcile her account. You will also write a check to make a credit card payment when the reconciliation is complete.

1. Ensure that the Chart of Accounts is open, click American Express, click Activities, and choose to reconcile the credit card account.

2. Using the following statement, reconcile the American Express account:

American Express
6539 Beck Place
New York, NY 07852

Credit Card Statement Prepared For:
Island Charters
3276 SW Maury Road
Maury, WA 98069

Account Number: 3333-888888-55555

Statement Period: April 28 - May 27, 2010

| Total Charges: | $434.11 | | Total Credits: | $33.75 |
| Beginning Balance: | $0.00 | | Ending Balance: | $400.36 |

Transactions:

Date	Description	Charge	Credit	Balance
	Beginning Balance			$0.00
5/1/2010	Thrifty Grocery	26.73		$26.73
5/4/2010	Dock Fuel Service	108.70		$135.43
5/6/2010	Malimali Hardware Store	43.20		$178.63
5/8/2010	The Boat Store	94.85		$273.48
5/11/2010	Thrifty Grocery	18.49		$291.97
5/14/2010	Dock Fuel Service	115.43		$407.40
5/17/2010	Sam's Service Station	26.71		$434.11
5/20/2010	The Boat Store		33.75	$400.36
	Periodic Finance Charge	0		$400.36
	Ending Balance			$400.36

3. When you have completed the reconciliation, choose to write a check to American Express for the entire amount using the next available check number and print a Summary Reconciliation Report.

Assessment 4.3 Answer Questions with Reports

Mary wants to answer the following questions. In this exercise, you will run the necessary reports to find answers and print each report for your instructor. Close QuickBooks when you are finished creating the reports.

1. How can I find out which transactions were not cleared when I reconciled my American Express account?

2. How can I print off a report showing all of the transactions affecting the American Express account?

3. How can I get a detailed list of all deposits for May?

4. Choose the appropriate option for your situation:

   ■ If you are continuing on to Lesson 5 or to the Critical Thinking exercises, leave Quick-Books open.

   ■ If you are finished working in QuickBooks, Choose File→Exit from the menu bar.

Critical Thinking

Critical Thinking 4.1   Sort Through the Stack

The owner of Griffin Construction has gotten behind on his QuickBooks entries again and has hired you to help him catch up. Restore Critical Thinking 4.1 from your file storage location and deal with the following "stack" of papers you found on the owner's desk. Use your best judgment in many cases to decide how to handle each item.

- Look at the following transactions recorded in a handwritten check register and enter them:

Date	Check #	Payee	Amount
05/15/10	1001	House Depot	$56.77
05/18/10	1002	Hakkman's Plumbing	$243.00
05/21/10	1005	Minch's Catering	$105.45
05/22/10	1003	Hitchcock Ford	$25.47
05/25/10	1004	Mama Dawn's Pizza	$34.86
05/30/10	1006	A.R. Hardware	$59.99

- A checking deposit slip for $150 with a sticky note on it: "Installed a door for Tom Jones"

- The following credit card receipts from a First American MasterCard account:
  - ◆ $25.46 to Pizza Porter for working lunch on 5/13/10
  - ◆ $78.93 to House Depot for job materials on 5/31/10
  - ◆ $114.68 to Hitchcock Ford for repair of company truck on 5/11/10
  - ◆ $32.56 to Sergeant's Fuel Stop for gas for company truck on 5/03/10
  - ◆ $250 to Glogowski Equipment Rental for jackhammer rental on 5/16/10
  - ◆ $50 from Glogowski Equipment Rental for return of deposit on 5/18/10

- This scribbled note: "Why isn't my Visa account showing up as a credit card in the Chart of Accounts?—Please fix."

Critical Thinking 4.2   Find a Reconciliation Error

David Hilson, the owner of Paradise Inn, has become very frustrated because he can't get his checking account to reconcile. He hires you as a QuickBooks consultant to get him on the right track. Restore the QuickBooks file Critical Thinking 4.2, print the Critical Thinking 4.2 Reconciliation report from your file storage location, and see if you can get David's account reconciled.

LESSON 5

Creating a Company

You have now mastered the basic customer, vendor, and banking activities required to use QuickBooks effectively. Now that you understand the basics, it is time to pull it all together and learn how to create a new QuickBooks company file. You will not have to start a company completely from scratch, as QuickBooks gives you a generic Chart of Accounts to start with and helps you in the setup process.

Beginning with this lesson, you will also work with account numbers in QuickBooks.

LESSON OBJECTIVES

After studying this lesson, you will be able to:

- Plan and create a company
- Customize a company file
- Edit your QuickBooks preferences
- Understand and enter opening balances and historical transactions
- Find help for QuickBooks
- Create QuickBooks users
- Create and use balance sheet reports

Integrative Case Study: Skortis Landscaping

You have been working with Skortis Landscaping's QuickBooks file for a while. You will now take a trip back in time and look at how the company was first created.

Before creating his new company, Justin thought about what he wanted QuickBooks to do for him. His friend told him that it is important to properly plan the QuickBooks company file in order to save time and increase efficiency in the future. The following is a checklist Justin wrote before he sat down to create the new QuickBooks company.

Company Info.

Skortis Landscaping
876 Main Street
Poway, CA 92064
Phone (858) 555-4589
Fax (858) 555-7856

Fiscal Yr. – January
Tax Yr. – January
Tax Form – 1040

Start Date – 04/30/10
Cash Basis

Federal EIN 99-9999999
State ID # 999-9999-9

Lists Needed:
~Chart of Accounts
Get from accountant

~Customers
Check for any existing balances
Payment terms

~Vendors
Find my account numbers
Payment terms
Outstanding bills

~Items
Ask accountant about these...
Services & Fees

Notice the type of information that Justin needed to gather before he began to set up his QuickBooks company file.

Planning & Creating a Company

Before you begin to set up your QuickBooks company, it is important to do some careful planning. You must think about the information you want to get from QuickBooks before you begin. As with many situations, garbage in will equal garbage out!

Choosing Your Start Date

Choosing the start date that is right for you is important. Very ambitious people may think they want to start their QuickBooks file the day they started their company. This is a nice idea, but not very practical for a busy or cost conscious entrepreneur.

Keep in mind that you must enter all transactions for your company (invoices, checks, bills paid, etc.) from the start date forward. If you choose a date too far in the past this process will take a long time to complete.

You should strive to start your QuickBooks company file at the beginning of a month, a quarter, or your fiscal year. You may want to discuss this matter with your accountant to help determine the best and most practical starting date for your business. The actual start date should be the last day of the prior period rather than the first day of the current period; for example, we will use 4/30/10 rather than 5/1/10.

The Five Ps

Sit down and think about what you want QuickBooks to do for you. It is hard to go back and add a new field for every customer or change every transaction! A little planning at the beginning can save you a lot of time in the future. Think about the five Ps as you get ready to start your company.

Prior
Planning
Prevents
Poor
Performance

One more thing to consider before creating your new company are all of the stakeholders involved. What type of information will each stakeholder need to be able to interact efficiently with your business? Potential stakeholders may include your accountant, customers, vendors, employees, stockholders, partners, etc.

How Many Companies Should You Create?

Generally, the best guideline is to set up a separate QuickBooks company file for each tax return you will file.

Creating a New QuickBooks File

There are several ways that you can go about creating your new QuickBooks file. Look at the following list to determine which one will work best for your situation:

- Create a company from scratch
- Upgrade from a previous version of QuickBooks
- Convert from a different QuickBooks edition
- Convert a Quicken file
- Convert a Peachtree© file

Choosing a Setup Path

When creating a new company from scratch, you must decide which path you want to take: EasyStep or Skip Interview.

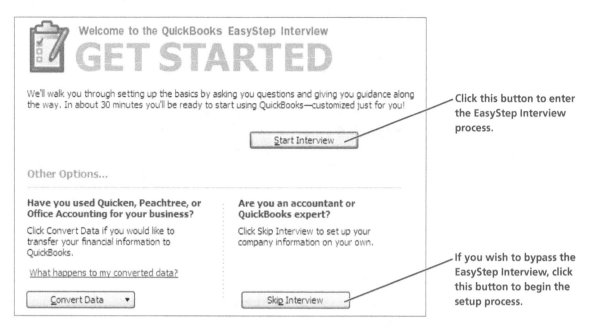

Click this button to enter the EasyStep Interview process.

If you wish to bypass the EasyStep Interview, click this button to begin the setup process.

When you choose to create a new company in QuickBooks, you will see this window, which allows you to choose the best method for you.

EasyStep

This method of company creation takes you through a series of questions. Your answer to each question determines how your company will be set up. The process is similar to Wizards in Microsoft products or Intuit's Turbo Tax program. Keep in mind that this method takes much longer and requires more in-depth planning. You will have the opportunity to use this method in the Skill Builder section of this lesson.

Skip Interview

If you don't want to go through the lengthy interview process, you can choose to skip it. QuickBooks will ask you for the basic information and it will be up to you to set up certain items such as payroll and inventory later. You will use this method in the hands-on exercises in this lesson.

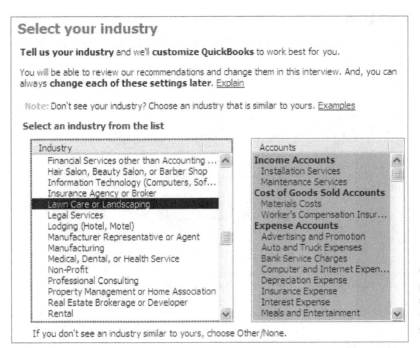

Select your industry

Tell us your industry and we'll **customize QuickBooks** to work best for you.

You will be able to review our recommendations and change them in this interview. And, you can always **change each of these settings later.** Explain

Note: Don't see your industry? Choose an industry that is similar to yours. Examples

Select an industry from the list

Industry	Accounts
Financial Services other than Accounting ...	**Income Accounts**
Hair Salon, Beauty Salon, or Barber Shop	Installation Services
Information Technology (Computers, Sof...	Maintenance Services
Insurance Agency or Broker	**Cost of Goods Sold Accounts**
Lawn Care or Landscaping	Materials Costs
Legal Services	Worker's Compensation Insur...
Lodging (Hotel, Motel)	**Expense Accounts**
Manufacturer Representative or Agent	Advertising and Promotion
Manufacturing	Auto and Truck Expenses
Medical, Dental, or Health Service	Bank Service Charges
Non-Profit	Computer and Internet Expen...
Professional Consulting	Depreciation Expense
Property Management or Home Association	Insurance Expense
Real Estate Brokerage or Developer	Interest Expense
Rental	Meals and Entertainment

If you don't see an industry similar to yours, choose Other/None.

QuickBooks has several predefined company files for specific industries that will help users in those or similar industries streamline their setup process.

TIP! *If you have one of the companies for which QuickBooks has already created a special predefined company file, it's a good idea to use it!*

A Setup Checklist

There are some items that you should gather before you begin to set up your company. Review the checklist of items to collect on the website for this course at labpub.com/learn/qb10_QC1/.

A Quick Payroll Primer

You will be introduced to running payroll in QuickBooks in *QuickBooks Pro 2010: Level 2*. If you choose to create your new company using the Easy Step interview method, you need to understand a bit about how QuickBooks deals with payroll first.

If you recall in Lesson 2, Working with Customer Transactions, you learned that if you want to include something on an invoice it must first be set up as an item. The same is true for payroll. If you wish to include an addition or deduction on an employee's paycheck you must first set it up as a payroll item. During the EasyStep interview you will have an opportunity to create payroll items. If you will be using QuickBooks for payroll and wish to set it up during the setup process, you will need to have the following information ready:

- Information for each employee: name, address, social security number, and withholding information (from their W-4).

- All "additions" that will be found on a paycheck, such as salaries, hourly wages, and bonuses.

- All payroll taxes the employees are required to pay.

- All payroll taxes you as the employer are required to pay.

- Any additional deductions you will be withholding from paychecks, such as investment plan contributions or child support payments.

Your Starter Chart of Accounts

During the setup process, QuickBooks will ask you to choose the business type that your company most closely resembles. QuickBooks will use your choice to create a Chart of Accounts close to what you need (it will take you less time to edit it to fit your unique business than to start from scratch). QuickBooks will also create profile lists based on your selection. You will work with the customer and vendor profile lists in *QuickBooks Pro 2010: Level 2*. Choose carefully here as you cannot go back and change the business type option.

!**WARNING!** *Once you select a business type during the setup process, you cannot change it later. You can edit and delete accounts and list entries, though.*

Account Beginning Balances

If you have an existing company for which you are setting up QuickBooks, you should enter the balances of all asset and liability accounts during the setup process (although you can enter them in the registers later). These account beginning balances are termed "opening balances" in QuickBooks. You will learn more about entering and editing these balances later in the lesson.

After you create your first balance sheet account, QuickBooks will create an Opening Balance Equity account, in which the account beginning balances you enter will be placed. Asset beginning balances credit the account and liability beginning balances debit it. This account is created so you can have a balance sheet that is accurate even if you haven't entered all assets and liabilities for your company.

TYPES OF ACCOUNTS IN QUICKBOOKS

Account Type	Example	Normal Balance
Bank	Checking Account	Debit
Accounts Receivable	Accounts Receivable	Debit
Other Current Asset	Prepaid Rent	Debit
Fixed Asset	Machinery	Debit
Other Asset	Long-Term Notes Receivable	Debit
Accounts Payable	Accounts Payable	Credit
Credit Card	Poway FNB Visa	Credit
Other Current Liability	Short-Term Loan	Credit
Long Term Liability	Auto Loan	Credit
Equity	Retained Earnings	Credit
Income	Sales	Credit
Cost of Goods Sold	Cost of Goods Sold	Debit
Expense	Telephone Expense	Debit
Other Income*	Interest Income	Credit
Other Expense*	Corporate Taxes	Debit

* Other income and other expense accounts are used to track income and expenses that are not the result of normal day to day business operations.

QUICK REFERENCE: CREATING A NEW COMPANY

Task	Procedure
Create a new company in QuickBooks	■ Go through the checklist to make sure you have all necessary information. ■ Plan what you want QuickBooks to do for you. ■ Choose File→New Company from the menu bar. ■ Choose the method you want to use to set up your company file in the EasyStep Interview window. ■ Complete the information QuickBooks needs to set up the company.
Edit information for a new company	■ Choose Company→Company Information from the menu bar. ■ Edit the information in the Company Information window.

Hands-On 5.1   Create a New Company

In this exercise, you will skip the EasyStep interview and set up the company for Skortis Landscaping.

 NOTE! *You will not need to open a portable company file in the beginning of this exercise as you did for previous lessons; you will create a new company instead.*

1. Launch QuickBooks.

2. Choose File→New Company from the menu bar.

3. Click the Skip Interview button.

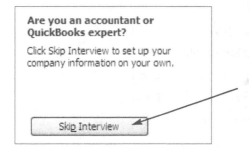

4. Follow these steps to enter the company information:

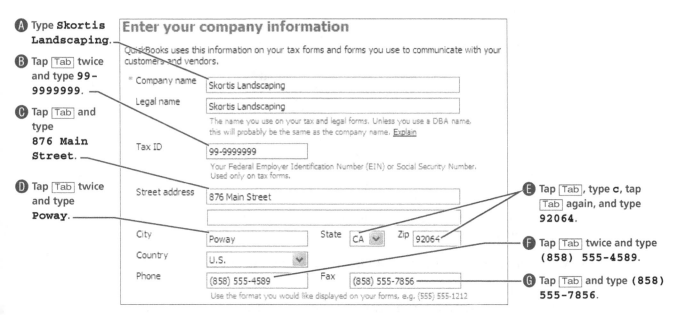

A Type **Skortis Landscaping.**

B Tap [Tab] twice and type **99-9999999.**

C Tap [Tab] and type **876 Main Street.**

D Tap [Tab] twice and type **Poway.**

E Tap [Tab], type **c**, tap [Tab] again, and type **92064.**

F Tap [Tab] twice and type **(858) 555-4589.**

G Tap [Tab] and type **(858) 555-7856.**

You will need to type the phone numbers just as you wish them to appear on forms in this window—including parentheses, dashes, and spaces. Be careful that you spell everything correctly when entering this company information. Imagine how embarrassing it would be to send out invoices, bills, and other correspondence with your own company name and information incorrect!

5. Click Next to continue with the new company setup.
   You can make future changes to this information by choosing Company→Company Information from the menu bar.

6. Click in the circle to choose Sole Proprietorship as the way in which your company is organized.

NOTE! *If you choose Other/None at this stage, you will not be able to assign tax lines to your accounts. This means you will not be able to transfer your tax information to tax preparation software or run income tax reports.*

7. Click Next twice, in the second screen selecting January as the first month of your fiscal year.

8. Click to choose Lawn Care or Landscaping as the company type that most closely matches yours.

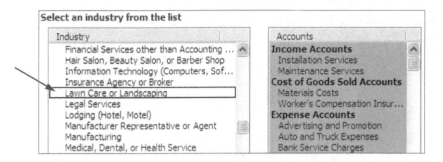

Take a moment to click the different company types on the left and view the resulting preset Chart of Accounts on the right.

9. Make sure that Lawn Care or Landscaping is chosen, and then click Next.

10. Click Next.
    QuickBooks will open a Filename for New Company window in which you will set where the new company file will be located as well as the name for the new file.

11. Follow these steps to save your new QuickBooks file:

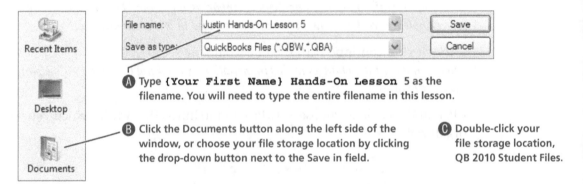

If you have not used the storage location described in Storing Your Exercise Files (the Documents folder), you will need to choose your unique storage location in step B.

For those using Windows XP or earlier, you will choose My Documents rather than Documents.

12. Click Save.
    Be patient here as it will take QuickBooks a few moments to set up the new file for you. You will see the Home page for the new company you just created.

13. Click the Finish button.

Editing Your QuickBooks Preferences

The way that you interact with QuickBooks is controlled by the preferences you select. The Preferences window has twenty-one categories of preferences you can set or modify so QuickBooks can work more efficiently for your company.

Notice the two tabs at the top of the window. They allow you to switch between company and personal preferences with a click of the mouse.

Along the left side of the Preferences window you can see the twenty-one categories of preferences.

Preferences	⬜
Accounting	

My Preferences   Company Preferences

☐ Pressing Enter moves between fields
☑ Automatically open drop-down lists when typing
☑ Beep when recording a transaction
☐ Automatically place decimal point
☑ Warn when editing a transaction

☐ Bring back all one time messages
☐ Turn off pop-up messages for products and services
☑ Show ToolTips for clipped text
☑ Warn when deleting a transaction or unused list item

Categories list:
Accounting, Bills, Checking, Desktop View, Finance Charge, **General**, Integrated Applications, Items & Inventory, Jobs & Estimates, Multiple Currencies, Payments, Payroll & Employees, Reminders, Reports & Graphs, Sales & Customers, Sales Tax, Send Forms, Service Connection, Spelling, Tax: 1099, Time & Expenses

Buttons: OK, Cancel, Help, Default

Also See:
Reminders

Automatically recall information
☑ Automatically remember account or transaction information
  ○ Automatically recall last transaction for this name
  ● Pre-fill accounts for vendor based on past entries

Default Date to Use for New Transactions
○ Use today's date as default   ● Use the last entered date as default

Keep custom item information when changing item in transactions
● Ask   ○ Always   ○ Never

Notice the many General preferences that each individual user can choose. Each option will affect how the individual interacts with QuickBooks.

Company vs. Personal Preferences

Each category has two tabs on which changes to preferences can be set: the Company Preferences tab and the My Preferences (personal) tab. Company preferences are controlled by the administrator and determine how the entire company interacts with QuickBooks. Personal preferences are controlled by each individual user and dictate interactions between Quick-Books and that one user only.

The following illustrations show an example of a company and a personal preference.

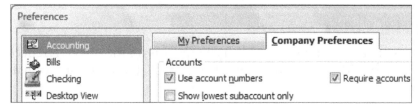

Preferences

Accounting / Bills / Checking / Desktop View

My Preferences   **Company Preferences**

Accounts
☑ Use account numbers   ☑ Require accounts
☐ Show lowest subaccount only

When the administrator makes a change to the company preference, it will affect how all users interact. In this example, the administrator turned on the preference to use account numbers, and in the Chart of Accounts there would now be an account number associated with each account.

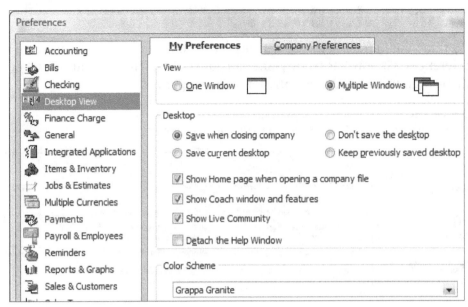

In this example, a user can make a change to the color scheme on the My Preferences tab that will affect only her individual QuickBooks user login. Notice the Show Coach window and features and Show Live Community preferences; these will be introduced later in this lesson.

Using Account Numbers

Many businesses use account numbers for the accounts in their Chart of Accounts. In the second half of this course, you will use account numbers. Account numbers are somewhat standard within the accounting world. "Somewhat" means that each account type begins with the same number, but the accounts listed within the account type are not universally numbered. Examine the following table to understand how account numbers work. Note that account numbers have a minimum of four characters, and you can use five or six. For instance, a Checking account (which is an asset) could be numbered 1000, 10000, or 100000. In this book we will be using five-digit account numbers.

Account number starts with:	Type of account	Example
1	Asset	Accounts Receivable
2	Liability	Credit Card
3	Equity	Retained Earnings
4	Income	Maintenance Services
5	Cost of Goods Sold	Materials Cost
6	Expenses	Telephone Expense
7	Other Income	Interest Income
8	Other Expense	Corporate Taxes

Changing the Color Scheme

The default color scheme is sea green. You can change this on the My Preferences tab of the Desktop View category. There are many color schemes available, and you can change your color scheme at any time.

Hands-On 5.2 Change Your Preferences

In this exercise, you will turn on the account number preference for the company and change the color scheme personal preference.

Turn On the Account Numbers Company Preference

Whether to turn on the use of account numbers is a company preference, is set by the company file administrator, and cannot be changed by other users.

1. Choose Edit→Preferences from the menu bar.

2. Follow these steps to turn on the account numbers preference:

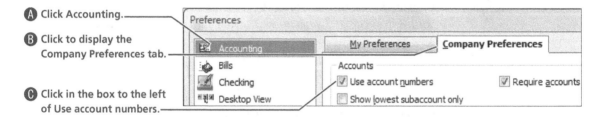

Ⓐ Click Accounting.

Ⓑ Click to display the Company Preferences tab.

Ⓒ Click in the box to the left of Use account numbers.

The Show lowest subaccount only preference will be introduced in QuickBooks Pro 2010: Level 2.

3. Click OK to accept the new preference.

Change a Desktop View Personal Preference

In this section, you will change the color scheme.

4. Choose Edit→Preferences from the menu bar.

5. Follow these steps to change your color scheme personal preference:

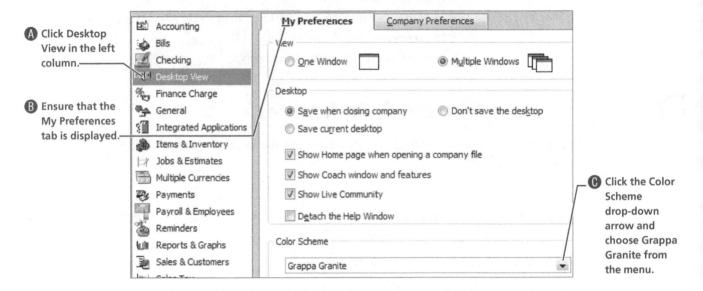

Ⓐ Click Desktop View in the left column.

Ⓑ Ensure that the My Preferences tab is displayed.

Ⓒ Click the Color Scheme drop-down arrow and choose Grappa Granite from the menu.

6. Click OK to accept the new preference.
   Take a look at the icon bar, and you can see the new purple color scheme displayed.

Customizing a Company File

During the setup process, QuickBooks allows you to choose a business type similar to your own. It is up to you to take this generic file and customize it to fit your company.

Modifying the Lists in a New File

You will need to look at several lists after you set up your new QuickBooks company to ensure that they are correct. If any of them are incorrect or incomplete, you will need to edit, delete, or add entries to them. These lists include the following:

- The Chart of Accounts
- The Customer & Job List
- The Vendor List
- The Item List
- The Fixed Asset Item List
- The Employee List
- The Payroll Items List

- The Price Level List

- Customer & Vendor Profile Lists

Entries in these lists can be created during the EasyStep interview. If you choose to skip the interview, you will need to populate these lists once the company has been created.

Customizing the Chart of Accounts

The first task you have with your new company file is to fine-tune your Chart of Accounts. If you are using QuickBooks for an existing business, you will want to talk to your accountant and get a copy of your current Chart of Accounts. If you are starting a new business, you may also want to contact your accountant for guidance on how to best set up your Chart of Accounts for your unique company.

Adding Accounts

Adding an account to your Chart of Accounts is much like adding a new item. Remember to make sure you select the correct account type, as this is one of the most prevalent errors accountants find in their clients' QuickBooks files. Keep in mind that your "behind the scenes" action will be incorrect if the wrong account type is selected.

To Edit or Delete—That Is the Question...

The generic Chart of Accounts that QuickBooks provides will have many accounts you probably won't need for your unique business. You can choose to either rename (edit) these accounts or delete them. Renaming an account is appropriate if you are working with the same account type. Deleting is appropriate if you no longer need additional accounts of the same type.

Moving and Sorting Accounts Within the List

You can change the order in which accounts appear within your Chart of Accounts. By default, QuickBooks alphabetizes the accounts by type. The Chart of Accounts is structured so that assets are listed first, liabilities second, equity accounts third, income accounts fourth, cost of goods sold accounts fifth, and expense accounts last. This structure must remain intact; you can only move accounts around within their own type.

If you move your accounts and later decide you want them alphabetized by type once again, QuickBooks allows you to re-sort the list. Re-sorting the list restores the QuickBooks default.

Subaccounts

To keep precise records, you may wish to use QuickBooks subaccounts. For instance, to keep the number of expense accounts within reason, you are likely to utilize only one telephone expense account for all of your telephone lines. To track expenses more closely, though, you may want to have separate accounts for your office phone, office fax, and cellular phone. Subaccounts are a great way to track these separate expenses while keeping the number of expense accounts down.

When you run P&L reports and budgets, you have the option to expand the report (show subaccounts) to show detail or collapse the report (show only main accounts) for brevity.

Expense			Expense		
60100 · Auto and Truck Expenses	75.59		60100 · Auto and Truck Expenses		75.59
60400 · Bank Service Charges	33.50		60400 · Bank Service Charges		33.50
62900 · Equipment Rental	300.00		62900 · Equipment Rental		300.00
63900 · Job Materials	51.15		63900 · Job Materials		51.15
64900 · Office Supplies	248.30		64900 · Office Supplies		248.30
66500 · Postage and Delivery	0.00		66500 · Postage and Delivery		0.00
67100 · Rent Expense	1,000.00		67100 · Rent Expense		1,000.00
68100 · Telephone Expense	509.94		68100 · Telephone Expense		
68600 · Utilities	213.48		68110 · Office Phone	319.02	
Total Expense	2,431.96		68120 · Fax Phone	48.76	
			68130 · Cell Phone	142.16	
			Total 68100 · Telephone Expense		509.94
			68600 · Utilities ▶		213.48 ◀
			Total Expense		2,431.96

On the left you can see the Expense section of a P&L report that is collapsed. On the right you can see the same report section expanded.

 NOTE! *A subaccount must be the same type of account as the main account.*

QR ▶ **QUICK REFERENCE: CUSTOMIZING THE CHART OF ACCOUNTS**

Task	Procedure
Move an account	■ Open the Chart of Accounts. ■ Click the account you want to move. ■ Place your mouse pointer over the diamond to the left of the account name until you see a four-way arrow. ■ Click and drag the account to the new location within the same account type.
Re-sort accounts	■ Open the Chart of Accounts. ■ Click the Account menu button. ■ Choose Re-sort List from the menu.
Create a subaccount	■ Open the Chart of Accounts. ■ Click the main account for which you wish to create a subaccount. ■ Click the Account menu button and choose New. ■ Choose the correct account type, and then click Continue. ■ Type the name of the subaccount. ■ Click in the box to the left of Subaccount of. ■ Click the drop-down arrow and select the main account from the list. ■ Click OK to accept the new subaccount.
Delete an account	■ Open the Chart of Accounts. ■ Single-click the account you want to delete. ■ Click the Account menu button. ■ Choose Delete from the menu. ■ Click OK to confirm the deletion.

In this exercise, you will take the generic Chart of Accounts created for Skortis Landscaping and make it fit the needs of the company.

Add an Account to the Chart of Accounts

The first task is to add an account that Justin needs, but that was not provided in the generic Chart of Accounts.

1. Click the Chart of Accounts task icon in the Company area of the Home page.
   QuickBooks opens the generic Chart of Accounts created for you. Notice the account numbers that you turned on in the previous exercise.

2. Click OK in the New Feature window.

3. Click the Account menu button at the bottom of the window and choose New from the menu.
   You will now set up Justin's checking account.

4. Follow these steps to create the new account:

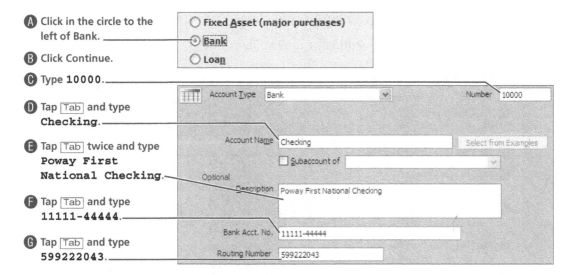

5. Click Save & Close to save the new account and close the Add New Account window. Click No in the Set Up Online Services window.

Edit an Account

In Lesson 2, Working with Customer Transactions, you used a service item called Installation that routed into an Installation Income account. QuickBooks created a similar account for you called Installation Services. You will now edit it to match the actual name you have chosen to use.

6. Scroll down the Chart of Accounts, if necessary, and then single-click the Installation Services account.

7. Click the Account menu button and choose Edit Account from the menu.

8. Follow these steps to finish renaming the account:

Ⓐ Delete the word *Services* and type **Income** in its place.

Ⓑ Click Save & Close.

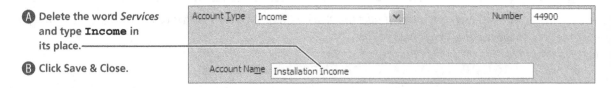

Delete an Account

9. Scroll to the bottom of the Chart of Accounts window and single-click the Ask My Accountant account.

10. Click the Account menu button and choose Delete Account from the menu.

11. Click OK in the Delete Account window.

Create Subaccounts

Justin has decided that he wants to track his telephone expenses more carefully and will use subaccounts.

12. Single-click Telephone Expense in the Chart of Accounts.

13. Click the Account menu button and choose New from the menu.

14. Follow these steps to add your new subaccount:

Ⓐ Click in the circle to the left of Expense.

Ⓑ Click Continue.

Ⓒ Type **68110** as the Number.

Ⓓ Tap Tab and type **Office Phone**.

Ⓔ Click in the box to the left of Subaccount of.

Ⓕ Tap Tab and type **t**; QuickBooks will fill in *Telephone Expense* for you.

Ⓖ Tap Tab and type **858-555-4589**.

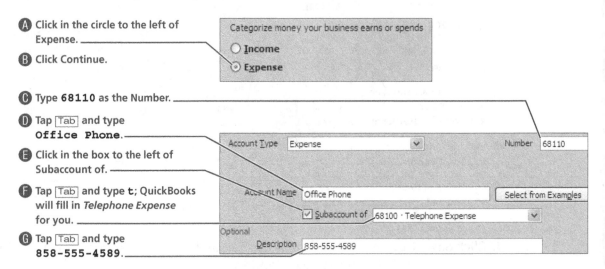

15. Click Save & New to add your next subaccount.

16. Follow substeps C through F from step 14 to add the following additional subaccounts for Telephone Expense, clicking Save & New after creating the first account:

Subaccount Name	Account Number	Description
Fax Phone	68120	858-555-4599
Cell Phone	68130	858-555-2976

17. Click Save & Close to accept the last new account and close the window.
    Look at your Chart of Accounts and notice the three subaccounts indented under the Telephone Expense account.

18. Close the Chart of Accounts window.

Opening Balances and Historical Transactions

If you chose a start date for your company that was not the first day that you were in business, it is important to enter all of the historical transactions and opening balances in your file.

Entering and Editing Account Opening Balances

You need to make sure that you have the correct opening balances in QuickBooks for all of your accounts. There are five different methods by which you can enter opening balances. The type of account that you are dealing with determines which method, or combination of methods, will work the best. The five methods available are:

- EasyStep Interview (for bank accounts only)

- Journal entries

- Forms (for individual transactions)

- Registers

- Lists (lump sums can be entered when creating entries)

Editing a Beginning Balance

If you need to correct a beginning balance that you entered, you will not be able to do it through the EasyStep Interview or the edit account window. In order to accomplish this task, you need to use either the account register or a journal entry (journal entries will be covered in *QuickBooks Pro 2010: Level 2*). For example, if you incorrectly entered $15,000 as the opening balance for the Savings account when you created it, you will need to open the Savings account register by double-clicking the account in the Chart of Accounts and change the amount in that window.

Entering Historical Transactions for an Account

There are two different ways that you can enter historical transactions into your QuickBooks file. Transactions can either be entered individually or in a summary journal entry.

Entering Historical Transactions Individually

If you wish to enter your transactions individually you must have all of the data for each one. It is very important that you enter them in the correct order. Check out the following illustration to see the correct order for historical transaction entry.

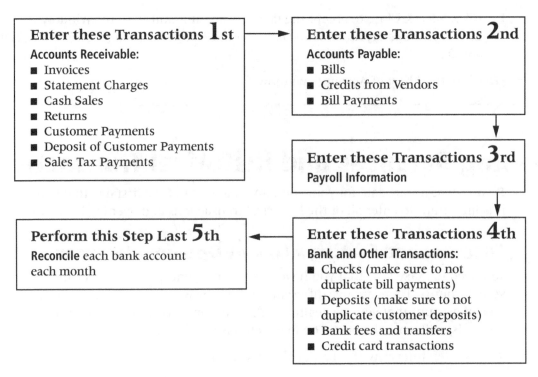

Enter these Transactions 1st

Accounts Receivable:
- Invoices
- Statement Charges
- Cash Sales
- Returns
- Customer Payments
- Deposit of Customer Payments
- Sales Tax Payments

Enter these Transactions 2nd

Accounts Payable:
- Bills
- Credits from Vendors
- Bill Payments

Enter these Transactions 3rd

Payroll Information

Enter these Transactions 4th

Bank and Other Transactions:
- Checks (make sure to not duplicate bill payments)
- Deposits (make sure to not duplicate customer deposits)
- Bank fees and transfers
- Credit card transactions

Perform this Step Last 5th

Reconcile each bank account each month

!TIP! *Remember that you must enter your historical information in the order displayed above!*

Entering a Summary Journal Entry

In a summary journal entry you will not enter the details of individual transactions, just the total amounts. Look at the following example:

The first three lines of this journal entry reflect invoices number 1–4, which are from the prior period.

The last four lines of this journal entry reflect checks numbered 997–1000.

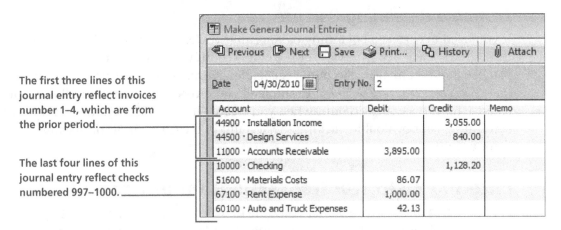

Notice that the debits (3,895+86.07+1,000+42.13=5,023.20) equal the credits (3,055+840+1,128.20=5,023.20).

You will learn how to make general journal entries in *QuickBooks Pro 2010: Level 2*. In this lesson, you will edit an opening balance in a register and enter a historical invoice on a form (Create Invoices).

QR **QUICK REFERENCE: ENTERING HISTORICAL TRANSACTIONS**

Task	Procedure
Edit an account opening balance	■ Open the register for the account.
	■ Drag to select the opening amount.
	■ Type the correct amount.
	■ Click Record.
Enter historical transactions individually	■ Gather the information together for all of the historical transactions.
	■ Enter all of your accounts receivable transactions using the proper QuickBooks forms (follow the order shown on page 162).
	■ Enter all of your accounts payable transactions using the proper QuickBooks forms (follow the order shown on page 162).
	■ Enter outstanding payroll information (for more information regarding payroll, see *QuickBooks Pro 2010: Level 2*).
	■ Enter outstanding "bank and other" transactions (follow the order shown on page 162).
	■ Reconcile each bank account for each month.
Enter a summary journal entry to account for historical transactions	■ Gather the information together for all of the historical transactions.
	■ Determine each account that is affected, whether the net effect is a debit or a credit, and the total amount.
	■ Choose Company→Make General Journal Entries from the menu bar.
	■ Enter each of the affected accounts and the amount of the debit/credit.
	■ Ensure that debits equal credits (QuickBooks will not allow you to record the journal entry until they do!).
	■ Record the journal entry.

 Hands-On 5.4 **Deal with Opening Balances and Historical Transactions**

In this exercise, you will work with both a register and a form to deal with historical transactions. You will begin by opening a portable company file that contains information required for the next four exercises.

Open a Portable Company File

The file you are about to open contains the transactions that you entered in the past three lessons.

1. Choose File→Open or Restore Company from the menu bar.

2. Open the Hands-On Lesson 5.4 QuickBooks portable company file from your file storage location, placing your name as the first word in the filename (e.g., Justin Hands-On Lesson 5.4).

Edit an Account Opening Balance

Justin made a mistake when he entered the opening balance for the Savings account, so you will need to help him change it.

3. Click the Check Register task icon in the Banking area of the Home page.

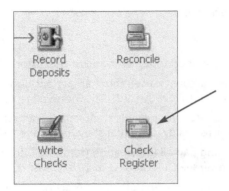

4. Click the drop-down arrow for the Select Account field, choose 10500•Savings from the list, and click OK.
QuickBooks will display the Savings account register.

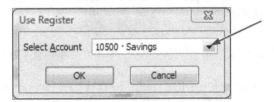

5. Drag to select the opening balance of $15,000 in the Deposit field and type **20000**.

6. Click the Record button at the bottom of the register window.

7. Click Yes when you see the Transaction Reconciled window.
When you enter an opening balance, QuickBooks will display it as being reconciled.

8. Close the Savings register window.

Use a Form to Enter Historical Transactions

If you need to enter a historical transaction that you would normally enter on a form, it is a good idea to enter it in the same form. In this case, you will create an invoice dated prior to the company's QuickBooks start date.

9. Choose Customers→Create Invoices from the menu bar.

10. Using the following information, create an invoice prior to your company start date:

Invoice number:	**3**
Customer:	**Sam Jones Construction, Bonita Park job**
Date:	**4/28/10**
Details:	**24 hours of Landscaping Installation work**
	8 hours of Landscape Design Services
Customer Message:	Choose whichever Customer Message you prefer

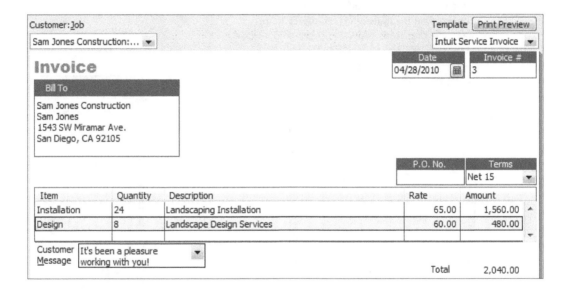

Your invoice should look similar to the one displayed above, which uses the Intuit Service Invoice. Notice that it doesn't matter in which order you enter the items on the invoice.

11. Click the Save & Close button to save the invoice and close the window.

Finding Help in QuickBooks

There will be times when you will need to be able to find answers to questions you have about QuickBooks on your own. QuickBooks has a built-in help feature as well as a "coaching" feature that can come to your rescue in these circumstances.

The QuickBooks Have a Question? Window

The QuickBooks Help window, which displays to the right of the main QuickBooks window when open, provides two tabs that allow you to find help:

- **The Live Community Tab**—Allows you to view questions that have been answered by other users, and to ask your own questions

- **The Help Tab**—Notice the subtabs that allow you to view topics relevant to what you are doing in QuickBooks, or to type a question or keyword(s) in order to search all words in the help topics

When using the Search tab, you search all of the words in the individual help topics. In this example, the words "How do I create a company file?" were typed into the help field.

The Back button allows you to return to the previous help topic viewed.

The Print Topic button allows you to print the help topic you are currently viewing.

The Live Community feature allows you to interact with other QuickBooks users in order to give and receive help.

NOTE! *The Maximize, Restore, and Minimize buttons for the main QuickBooks window control the Have a Question? window as well.*

Once you find the topic you are searching for, QuickBooks allows you to easily print the information by clicking the Print Topic button on the toolbar above the topic title. Or, you can "go green" and save save paper by just viewing the topic displayed to the right of your QuickBooks window as you work through the topic.

After you click the Ask a Question button, QuickBooks will go online and look for similar questions that have already been answered. Those answers will be displayed in a Live Community window. If you don't find the answer you need, you can post your question to the online community of QuickBooks users.

The QuickBooks Coach

The QuickBooks Coach is a feature that helps guide QuickBooks users who are either new to the program or who are upgrading to the new version. It demonstrates how the business flows on the Home page and uses tips and "spotlights" that explain the tasks involved. It also demonstrates how to improve your work and how different tasks work together for your business within the workflow. For seasoned users, the Coach also provides a tutorial that demonstrates the new features of the 2010 software. In addition, if you choose to "Get Set Up", you will be taken online to learn about how you can sign up for fee-based support services.

When you create a new company, the QuickBooks Coach appears in the upper-right corner of the Home page. It can either stay as a part of the Home page, or you can maximize it so that it is a separate "floating" window. You can choose to display or hide it at any time by going to the Desktop View category of your Preferences, which you learned about earlier in this lesson.

The QuickBooks Coach provides assistance for those new to the program who are not sure where to begin, as well as for those who are familiar with the program and who might benefit from a little coaching along the way.

QUICK REFERENCE: FINDING HELP IN QUICKBOOKS

Task	Procedure
Search for help by browsing relevant topics	■ Choose Help→QuickBooks Help from the menu bar. ■ Click the Help tab. ■ Click the Relevant Topics sub tab. ■ When you see the topic you desire, scroll down (if necessary) and click it to display the help topic in the bottom portion of the window.
Search for help by searching the text of the entire help topics	■ Choose Help→QuickBooks Help from the menu bar. ■ Click the Help tab. ■ Click the Search sub tab. ■ Type the question you have about QuickBooks and tap ⌨Enter. ■ Look at the Search Results displayed, and then click the topic about which you wish to learn more.
Print a help topic	■ Search for the topic of your choice by using either the Relevant Topics or Search sub tab. ■ Click the Print Topic button on the toolbar. ■ Set your printer and print options, and then click Print.
Turn on/off the QuickBooks Coach feature	■ Choose Edit→Preferences from the menu bar. ■ Display the Desktop View category. ■ Display the My Preferences tab. ■ Click to select/deselect "Show Coach window and features".

In this exercise, you will use two of the help features in QuickBooks.

Search for Help

You will begin by using the QuickBooks help feature to learn how to create a new company file.

1. Choose Help→QuickBooks Help from the menu bar if the Have a Question? window is not displayed.

2. Follow these steps to search for a help topic:

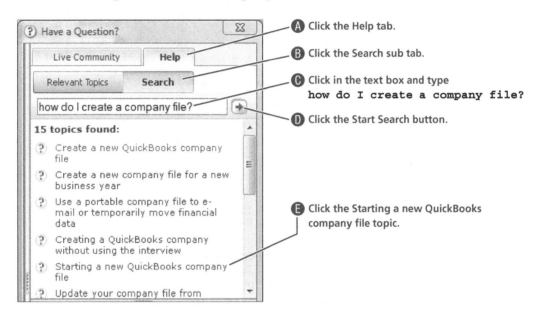

Ⓐ Click the Help tab.

Ⓑ Click the Search sub tab.

Ⓒ Click in the text box and type **how do I create a company file?**

Ⓓ Click the Start Search button.

Ⓔ Click the Starting a new QuickBooks company file topic.

The topic you chose will be displayed in the bottom area of the Help window.

3. Take a look at the bottom section of the Help window, scrolling down if necessary, and read the entire topic.

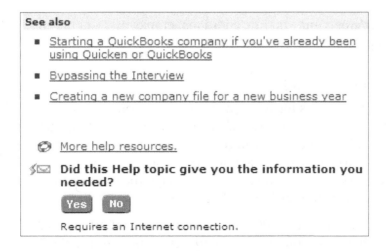

Notice that if you did not find the exact topic you were looking for, QuickBooks provides you with links to related topics and resources.

Access the Live Community

You can also rely on other QuickBooks users to help you out by looking at questions that have already been answered and/or posting one of your own. (You will need a live Internet connection to complete this exercise.)

4. Follow these steps to ask a question of the community of QuickBooks users:

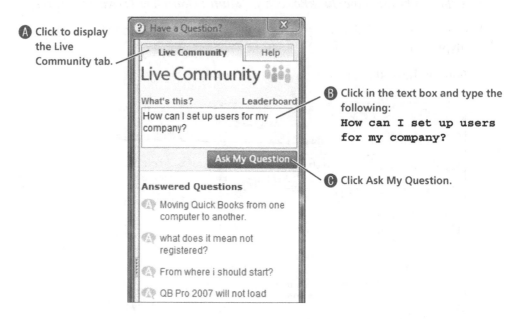

A Click to display the Live Community tab.

B Click in the text box and type the following:

How can I set up users for my company?

C Click Ask My Question.

Take a look at the questions that have been answered that are similar to yours.

5. Click the I Found My Answer button.
   You will be returned to the QuickBooks Home page.

Setting Up Users

When your company grows and you hire additional employees, you may decide that you need to allow certain employees access to your QuickBooks file.

Administrators and Users

Before you can set up any users for your QuickBooks file, you must set up an administrator who will control the access of all users. You can assign a password for each person with access to your file. The administrator controls all company preferences in the Preferences window. Users have the ability to change only their own personal preferences. QuickBooks allows you to set up unlimited users for your company file, although the number that can access the file at any one time depends on your QuickBooks license agreement.

A user type that was introduced in 2009, the External Accountant, has access to all areas of QuickBooks except those that contain confidential customer information. An External Accountant can conduct reviews of your file and separate the changes from those of other users. Only an adminstrator can create an External Accountant user.

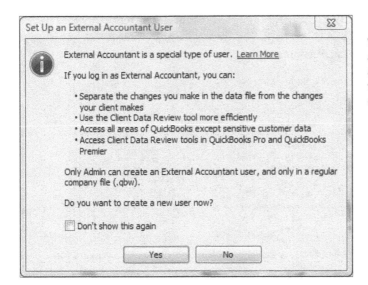

When you open a QuickBooks file, the Set Up an External Accountant User window will appear, allowing you to easily set up this user type. Note the checkbox you can select in order to not see this window appear again.

Restricting Access

When you decide to give employees access to your QuickBooks company file, you may not want them to see all of your company's financial information. You can choose to restrict each individual user's access to specific areas of QuickBooks.

There are nine areas for which you can give access rights to a user. The following illustration displays those areas. In this example, Tammy has access to all areas of sales and accounts receivable (creating new transactions, printing forms, and running reports) and can create new purchase and accounts payable transactions.

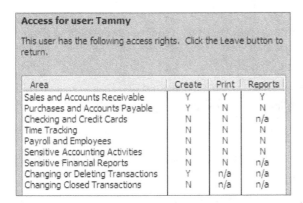

Access for user: Tammy

This user has the following access rights. Click the Leave button to return.

Area	Create	Print	Reports
Sales and Accounts Receivable	Y	Y	Y
Purchases and Accounts Payable	Y	N	N
Checking and Credit Cards	N	N	n/a
Time Tracking	N	N	N
Payroll and Employees	N	N	N
Sensitive Accounting Activities	N	N	N
Sensitive Financial Reports	N	N	n/a
Changing or Deleting Transactions	Y	n/a	n/a
Changing Closed Transactions	N	n/a	n/a

Setting Passwords

It is very important to make sure you have a password that is not easy for others to guess and yet that is easy for you to remember. Once you set your username and password, the Change QuickBooks Password window allows you to change your password whenever you wish (recommended every 90 days) and to set or change your secret "challenge question" that will allow you to retrieve a forgotten password. This challenge question should not have an answer with which others are familiar.

Change user password and access	⊠

Admin Name and Password

Provide a name and an optional password for this user.

User Name:	Kathleen
Password:	••••••
Confirm Password:	••••••

Select a challenge question and enter answer.

How will this help me recover my password?

Challenge Question:	Your high school mascot ▾
Challenge Answer:	••••••

In the Change QuickBooks Password window, you can change your username and password for the file and set a challenge question that will help you reset your password if you forget it.

QUICK REFERENCE: SETTING UP USERS AND PASSWORDS

Task	Procedure
Set up an administrator name and password	■ Choose Company→Set Up Users and Passwords→Set Up Users. ■ Select Admin and click Edit User. ■ Type the username and password, entering the password twice to verify. ■ Choose a challenge question, if desired. ■ Type the challenge question answer, if necessary. ■ Click OK.
Change an administrator password	■ Choose Company→Set Up Users and Passwords→Change Your Password from the menu bar. ■ Type a complex password; retype it to verify you did it correctly. ■ Choose a challenge question, if desired. ■ Type the challenge question answer, if necessary. ■ Click OK.
Set up users	■ Choose Company→Set Up Users and Passwords→Set Up Users. ■ Click Add User. ■ Type the username and password and click Next. ■ Follow the steps in the "Set up user password and access" screens to customize the access for the user. ■ View the new user's access rights and click Finish.

Hands-On 5.6   Set Up Users for a Company

In this exercise, you will help Kathleen set up Tammy (a future employee) as a user for the Skortis Landscaping company file.

Set Up an Administrator Password

Before Kathleen sets Tammy up as a user, she needs to set her own password as the administrator.

1. Choose Company→Set Up Users and Passwords→Set Up Users from the menu bar.

2. Click Edit User to change the name and set a password for the Admin account.

3. Follow these steps to set up Kathleen's administrator account and password:

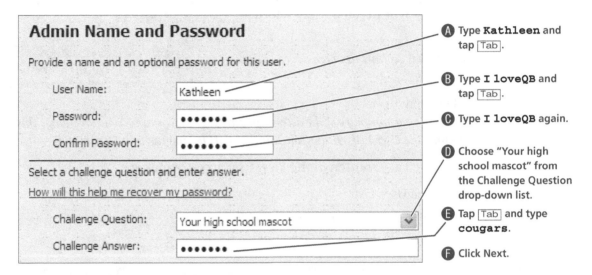

4. Click Finish.
   Notice that you do not need to change the access areas for the administrator. She has access to everything in the company file!

Add a User

Now that the administrator is set up, you can set up the individual users.

5. Click the Add User button in the User List window, and then follow these steps to add Tammy as a user:

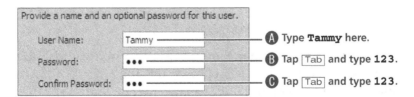

6. Click Next twice.
   Each time you click Next as you move through the "Set up user password and access" screens, you can change the access for the user in one of nine areas.

7. Click to choose the Full Access for Sales and Accounts Receivable option, and then click Next.

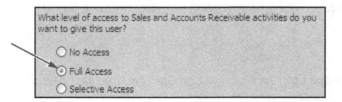

8. Click in the circle to the left of Selective Access for Purchases and Accounts Payable. The Create transactions only option will be automatically selected.

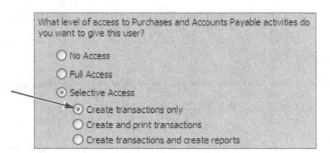

9. Click Finish.
   Notice that Tammy has been added to the User List.

10. Click View User.
    You will see a summary of the access you have given to Tammy. You can change this at any time by opening the User List, clicking on Tammy, and clicking the Edit User button.

11. Click the Leave button in the View user access window.

12. Close the User List.

Working with the Balance Sheet Report

In Lesson 3, Working with Vendor Transactions, you learned how to produce one of the main company reports, the P&L report. In this section, you will look at another vital report, the balance sheet report.

Types of Accounts Displayed

A balance sheet report displays all of your asset, liability, and equity accounts (hence the designation the "balance sheet accounts"). You can customize your report to show only the accounts you wish to display.

Memorizing Reports

Once you have created a report with your chosen accounts, you may wish to save the report settings so you can easily produce the same report again. The process of saving the settings of a report is called memorizing a report and it is available for all reports. The memorizing feature memorizes the format of the report, not the data contained within it. This means that when you open a memorized report, it will be comprised of your most recently entered data.

To recall the memorized report, you can choose it from the Memorized Report List.

Filtering Reports

In order to have reports display only certain pieces of data, you have the ability to apply a filter in QuickBooks. A filter will let you choose what information to include in your report, thereby "filtering out" the rest of it. Filters can be applied to any report, and the specific information that can be filtered is determined by the report you run.

Accrual vs. Cash Basis Reporting

If you recall from Lesson 1, Introducing QuickBooks Pro, there are two methods of accounting you can choose for your company. Regardless of which method you choose, QuickBooks doesn't require you to enter information any differently. QuickBooks allows you to easily change your reports to view either method. When you first create a QuickBooks company, the default will be for the reports to be displayed as the accrual basis. Take a look at a review of both methods:

Accrual Basis

In the accrual basis of accounting, income is recorded when a sale is made and expenses are recorded when accrued. This method is used often by firms and businesses with large inventories.

Cash Basis

In the cash basis of accounting, income is recorded when cash is received and expenses are recorded when cash is paid. This method is commonly used by small businesses and professionals.

If you operate using the cash basis, you will not need to display Accounts Receivable and Accounts Payable on your financial statements since cash has yet to change hands.

Company Snapshot

The Company Snapshot window gives you a quick view of your company's bottom line in one convenient place. You can customize it to include "at-a-glance" reports that are the most important to your company. The Company Snapshot can be accessed via a button on the icon bar or by choosing Reports→Company Snapshot from the menu bar. The Company Snapshot will show information only within a preset date range. If you don't see anything displayed, it is likely because the date for which you are performing the exercise is past the date range available through the snapshot.

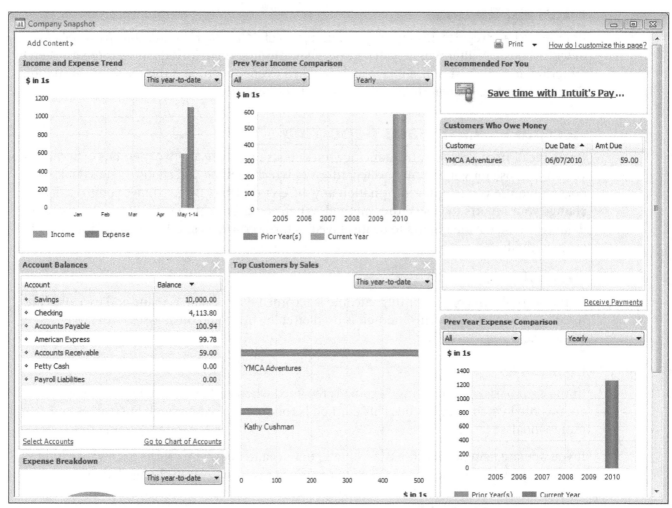

The Company Snapshot allows you to graphically see information about your company and get broad overall view of where you stand.

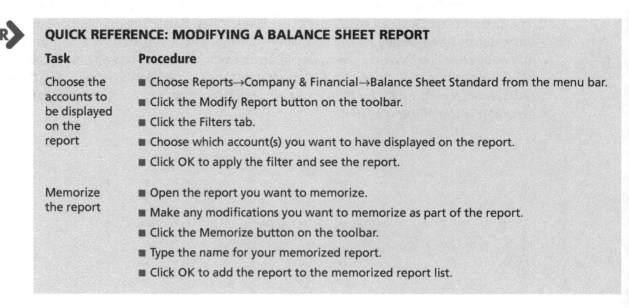

QUICK REFERENCE: MODIFYING A BALANCE SHEET REPORT

Task	Procedure
Choose the accounts to be displayed on the report	■ Choose Reports→Company & Financial→Balance Sheet Standard from the menu bar. ■ Click the Modify Report button on the toolbar. ■ Click the Filters tab. ■ Choose which account(s) you want to have displayed on the report. ■ Click OK to apply the filter and see the report.
Memorize the report	■ Open the report you want to memorize. ■ Make any modifications you want to memorize as part of the report. ■ Click the Memorize button on the toolbar. ■ Type the name for your memorized report. ■ Click OK to add the report to the memorized report list.

QUICK REFERENCE: MODIFYING A BALANCE SHEET REPORT (CONTINUED)

Task	Procedure
Recall a memorized report	■ Choose Reports→Memorized Reports→Memorized Report List from the menu bar. ■ Double-click the memorized report you wish to run.
Change the basis of the report	■ Produce your desired report or recall it from the Memorized Report List. ■ Click the Modify Report button on the toolbar. ■ Click in the circle to the left of Accrual or Cash, depending on which basis you wish to use. ■ Click OK to produce the revised report.

 Hands-On 5.7   Run a Balance Sheet Report

In this exercise, you will create a balance sheet report that displays all of your asset, liability, and equity accounts.

Create and Customize a Balance Sheet Report

First you will create the balance sheet report and select which accounts you want displayed.

1. Choose Reports→Company & Financial→Balance Sheet Standard from the menu bar.

2. Tap [a] to set All as your date range.

3. Follow these steps to create a balance sheet that only shows your assets:

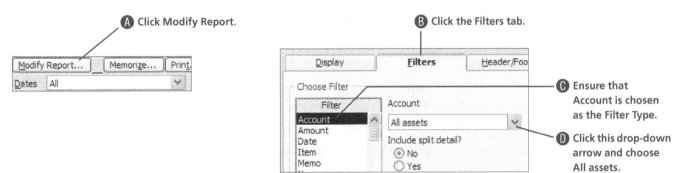

Ⓐ Click Modify Report.

Ⓑ Click the Filters tab.

Ⓒ Ensure that Account is chosen as the Filter Type.

Ⓓ Click this drop-down arrow and choose All assets.

4. Click OK to apply the report settings.
   Your report should display only the asset accounts; notice the amount in the Checking account: $4,099.54.

Memorize a Balance Sheet Report

Now you will memorize the report with the changes you made (changing the date range to all and displaying only the asset accounts).

5. Click the Memorize button on the report toolbar.

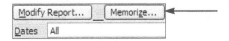

6. Type **Assets Only Balance Sheet, All Dates**.

Name:	Assets Only Balance Sheet, All Dates
☐ Save in Memorized Report Group:	Accountant

7. Click OK to memorize the report.

8. Close the report window.
   Remember that there was $4,099.54 in the Checking account when the report was memorized. You will now write a check and see how it affects the memorized report once it is recalled.

9. Click the Write Checks task icon in the Banking area of the Home page.

10. Follow these steps to write a check for supplies:

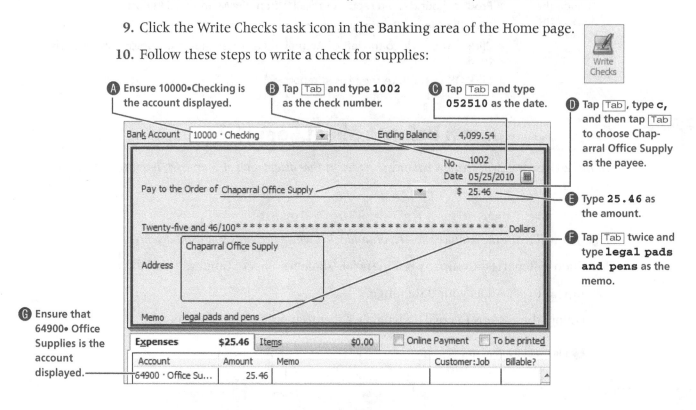

Ⓐ Ensure 10000•Checking is the account displayed.

Ⓑ Tap Tab and type **1002** as the check number.

Ⓒ Tap Tab and type **052510** as the date.

Ⓓ Tap Tab, type **c**, and then tap Tab to choose Chaparral Office Supply as the payee.

Ⓔ Type **25.46** as the amount.

Ⓕ Tap Tab twice and type **legal pads and pens** as the memo.

Ⓖ Ensure that 64900• Office Supplies is the account displayed.

Notice how the expense account automatically fills in for you because it was used last time for this vendor. The account number and account name also now show up in the account column because you have turned on the account number preference.

11. Click Save & Close to record the transaction and close the window.

Recall a Memorized Report

You have made changes (added a transaction) since you memorized the Assets Only Balance Sheet report; you will now recall it and see how QuickBooks dealt with the change.

12. Choose Reports→Memorized Reports→Assets Only Balance Sheet, All Dates from the menu bar.
    Look at the Checking account amount—it now reflects the transaction you just entered.

13. Double-click with the QuickZoom pointer on the Checking amount ($4,074.08).
    The Transactions by Account report will show all transactions that have led to this balance. Notice that check #1002 is reflected in the memorized report.

14. Close the Transactions by Account report window.

Switch Between Accrual and Cash Basis for a Report

By default, QuickBooks creates reports based on the accrual basis of accounting (until you change the preference). Look at the balance sheet report and notice the Accounts Receivable account. You will now change the report to reflect the cash basis method.

15. Click the Modify Report button on the report tool bar.

16. Click in the circle to the left of Cash in the Report Basis section of the window.

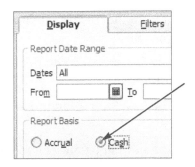

17. Click OK to make the change to the report.
    Notice that Accounts Receivable is no longer displayed since you have yet to receive the cash.

18. Choose Window→Close All from the menu bar.

19. Click No to not memorize the change to the report.

20. Choose the appropriate option for your situation:

    ■ If you are continuing on to the end-of-lesson exercises, leave QuickBooks open and complete the Concepts Review section.

    ■ If you are finished working in QuickBooks, Choose File→Exit from the menu bar.

Concepts Review

True/False Questions

1. You should always set your QuickBooks start date to be the first day you started your business.   TRUE   FALSE

2. The five Ps teach you to plan your company well initially to avoid problems in the future.   TRUE   FALSE

3. The EasyStep Interview is a quick company setup method that only asks you for the basics.   TRUE   FALSE

4. The normal balance of an income account is a debit balance.   TRUE   FALSE

5. Liabilities are always listed first in the Chart of Accounts.   TRUE   FALSE

6. Preferences control the way you interact with the QuickBooks program.   TRUE   FALSE

7. You should create a separate QuickBooks company file for each tax return you file.   TRUE   FALSE

8. A subaccount must always be an expense, regardless of the main account type.   TRUE   FALSE

9. If you choose to skip the EasyStep Interview, you can set up additional features at a later date.   TRUE   FALSE

10. You have to re-memorize a report each time you enter new data.   TRUE   FALSE

Multiple Choice Questions

1. With what number would an income account start once you turn on the account numbers preference?
   a. 2
   b. 3
   c. 4
   d. 5

2. Which of the following accounts would show a credit normal balance?
   a. Auto Loan
   b. Prepaid Insurance
   c. Checking
   d. Rent Expense

3. Which of these can you *not* change in the Preferences window?
   a. Use of account numbers
   b. Use of English or Spanish language
   c. Whether to display reminders
   d. Turn on the inventory feature

4. Which account would you find on a balance sheet report?
   a. Payroll Liabilities
   b. Utilities Expense
   c. Sales
   d. Cost of Goods Sold

Skill Builders

Skill Builder 5.1   Set Up a New QuickBooks Company

In this exercise, you will use the EasyStep Interview to set up the company for The Tea Shoppe at the Lake.

1. If necessary, open QuickBooks.

2. Choose File→New Company from the menu bar.

3. Click the Start Interview button on the Easy Step Interview screen.

4. Refer to the information on the following page to complete the EasyStep Interview for Susie.
   Once you reach the end of the interview you will see a "Congratulations!" screen.

5. Click Finish to complete the interview.
   A QuickBooks window explaining the new online services available with QuickBooks 2010 launches.

6. Click Remind Me Later in the Intuit Account window.

7. Click the Close button on the QuickBooks Coach window to anchor it to the upper-right portion of the Home page.

EASY STEP INTERVIEW INFORMATION

Field	Data
Company/Legal Name	The Tea Shoppe at the Lake
Tax ID (Federal Employee Identification Number)	99-9999999
Address	316 Swan Drive Lake San Marcos, CA 92078
Phone	(760) 555-3759
Fax	(760) 555-3758
Industry Type	Restaurant, Caterer, or Bar
Company Organization	S Corporation
First Month of Fiscal Year	January
Administrator Password	Tea4two (Remember that passwords are case-sensitive.)
File Name	{Your First Name} Skill Builder 5 (e.g., Susie Skill Builder 5)
What Is Sold?	Services Only
Sales Tax	No
Estimates	No
Sales Receipts	Yes
Billing Statements	Yes
Invoices	Yes
Progress Invoicing	No
Bill Tracking	Yes
Print Checks	I print checks.
Credit Cards	I don't currently accept credit cards, but I would like to.
Time Tracking	No
Employees	No
Multiple Currencies	No
Start Date	04-30-2010
Bank Account	Add Bank Account - Checking, #555-777, routing # 200300400, opened before 04/30/10, statement ending date 04/23/10, ending balance $23,000
Income & Expense Accounts	Start with the accounts provided

Skill Builder 5.2　Customize Your File

In this exercise, you will customize the file you just created for The Tea Shoppe.

Before you begin: Make sure you have completed Skill Builder 5.1.

Turn On the Account Number Preference

You will begin by turning on the account number preference so that when you create and edit accounts you can enter the numbers.

1. Choose Edit→Preferences from the menu bar.

2. Choose the Accounting category.

3. Click the Company Preferences tab.

4. Click in the box to turn on the Use account numbers preference.

5. Click OK.

Add a New Account

Susie wants to add her Kirkland Visa account.

6. Choose Lists→Chart of Accounts from the menu bar.

7. Click the Account menu button and choose New.
   The account menu button can be found in the bottom-left area of the Chart of Accounts window.

8. Choose Credit Card as the account type, and click Continue.

9. Type **20500** in the Number field, tap [Tab], and type **Kirkland Visa** as the Name.

10. Click Save & Close. Click No in the Set Up Online Services window.

Edit an Account

Susie needs to add the account number to the Checking account.

11. Scroll up and right-click on Checking, and then choose Edit Account from the shortcut menu.

12. Type **10000** in the Number field and click Save & Close.

Delete an Account

Susie has decided that she doesn't need the Uniforms expense account, so you will delete it for her.

13. Scroll down, if necessary, and single-click on account 68500•Uniforms.

14. Click the Account menu button and choose Delete Account. Click OK to confirm the deletion.

Add Subaccounts

You will now add two subaccounts for the Professional Fees account: Chamber and Rotary.

15. Click the Account menu button and choose New.

16. Choose Expense as the account type, and click Continue.

17. Enter **66705** as the Number and **Conferences** as the Name.

18. Make it a subaccount of 66700•Professional Fees.

19. Click Save & New, and then create one additional subaccount for Professional Fees: 66710•Certification.

20. Click Save & Close, and close the Chart of Accounts window.

Skill Builder 5.3   Produce a Balance Sheet Report

Susie wants to run a balance sheet report. You will open a portable company file so that the report contains the data from the first four lessons.

1. Restore the Skill Builder 5.3 portable company file from your default file location, placing your name as the first word in the filename (e.g., Susie Skill Builder 5.3).

2. Choose Reports→Company & Financial→Balance Sheet Standard from the menu bar.

3. Tap ⓐ to change the date range to All.

4. Apply a filter so that the report will show only Liabilities.

5. Memorize the report as **Liability Report**.

6. Choose Window→Close All from the menu bar.

7. Open the memorized Liability Report and print it for your instructor.

8. Close the report window, and then close QuickBooks.

 # Assessments

Assessment 5.1 Create and Customize a New Company File

In this exercise, you will go back in time to help Mary create her QuickBooks company file. You will not need to open a portable company file as you will create a new company file for Island Charters. You should use the Skip Interview method to set up your company.

1. Use the following information to set up a new company file for Mary:

Company/Legal Name	Island Charters
Tax ID Number	99-9999999
Address	3276 SW Maury Road Maury, WA 98069
Phone #	(206) 555-7534
FAX #	(206) 555-7535
Income tax form	Form 1040 (Sole Proprietor)
Fiscal Year first month	January
Company Type	General Service-based Business
File name	{Your First Name} Assessment 5

2. Choose to be reminded later about online services.

3. Close the QuickBooks Learning Center window, if necessary.

4. Open the Chart of Accounts and add the following accounts: Checking (Bank), Savings (Bank), American Express (Credit Card), Charter Income (Income), and Boat Fuel (Expense).

5. Delete the Travel Expense account, and then close the Chart of Accounts window.

Assessment 5.2 Change Account Preferences

You will now set the preferences so that QuickBooks functions just as Mary desires.

1. Open the Preferences window.

2. Change the color scheme to Denim Blues.

3. Choose to have QuickBooks show the To Do Notes when you open a new company file.
   Hint: Look in the Reminders category.

4. Choose to turn off pop-up messages for products and services.
   Hint: Look in the General category.

Assessment 5.3   Create and Recall a Memorized Report with a Filter

You will need to open a portable company file to complete this exercise.

1. Open the Assessment 5.3 portable company file from your default file location and place your name as the first word in the filename (e.g., Mary Assessment 5.3). Click Cancel if the Create a Backup window appears.

2. Create an Expenses By Vendor Detail report.

3. Change the date range to All and change the basis for just this report to Cash.

4. Choose for the report to display only Dock Fuel Service transactions.
   Hint: Apply a Filter by Name.

5. Memorize the report, name it **Dock Fuel Service Expenditures**, and then close it.

6. Enter a charge on your American Express card dated 5/31/10 for $97.84 of boat fuel payable to Dock Fuel Service.

7. Recall the memorized report, Dock Fuel Service Expenditures.

8. Choose the appropriate option for your situation:
   - If you are continuing on to the Critical Thinking exercises, leave QuickBooks open.
   - If you are finished working in QuickBooks, Choose File→Exit from the menu bar.

Critical Thinking

Critical Thinking 5.1   Decide Whether to Re-Create or Not

You have just started a new job as the bookkeeper for a florist shop. The owner tried to set up QuickBooks on her own, but she isn't sure if she did it correctly. Take a look at the QuickBooks company file that she set up and tell her whether it would be wiser to start over with a new company file or to make adjustments to the existing file. She has entered a month worth of transactions that would have to be reentered if you re-created the file.

Launch QuickBooks. Open the Critical Thinking 5.1 file. Examine how it was set up and the number of entries made. Determine whether it would be better for you to correct the existing file or recreate the file and reenter the transactions. Using a word processing program, type your response to the owner of the company and state why you reached your decision. Save the document as **Critical Thinking 5.1** and submit it to your instructor for review.

Critical Thinking 5.2   Decide Which Basis Makes More Sense

You have decided to work for yourself and have opened a welding shop. You bill your customers Net 30 and have the same terms with most of your vendors. You are trying to decide if you want to operate your business under the cash or accrual basis. In QuickBooks you will enter all transactions the same regardless of which basis you choose. However, your reports will be different based on your decision.

Decide which accounting basis you will use for your business. Type your answer in a word processing program and make sure to provide supporting evidence as to why you made the decision that you did. Save the document as **Critical Thinking 5.2** and submit it to your instructor for review.

Need to Know Accounting

Even though QuickBooks does everything for you "behind the scenes," it is important that you have a basic understanding of what is happening to your books.

In this appendix, you will learn about the basic financial statements important to any business and the accounts that appear on these reports. You will also learn about the double-entry accounting system and the debits and credits that must always be equal.

In This Appendix

Topic	Description	See Page
Working with Financial Statements	A discussion of the balance sheet and income statement, and the accounts found on each report	188
Debits and Credits: The Double-Entry Accounting System	An analysis of the accounting rule that states that debits must equal credits	191
Finding Additional Accounting Resources	Where to find online information on accounting concepts	193

Working with Financial Statements

There are two main reports that a company will produce periodically to illustrate its financial well-being.

- A **Balance Sheet** report displays all of the holdings of the company along with the debts as of a particular date.

- An **Income Statement**, otherwise known as a Profit & Loss Report, displays the income and expenses for a specified period of time.

Understanding the accounts that make up each of these reports is key to understanding your company's books.

The Accounting Equation and the Balance Sheet

The first equation you need to learn when it comes to accounting is simply termed the accounting equation:

$$\text{Assets} = \text{Liabilities} + \text{Equity}$$

This means that if you take all of your company's debt and add any investments (equity), you will have a value equal to all of the assets that your company owns.

A balance sheet is a financial statement that displays all asset, liability, and equity accounts (the balance sheet accounts). Take a look at the following illustrations to see how the accounting equation works and is represented in a balance sheet:

The upper section of the balance sheet represents the left side of the accounting equation and displays all of the assets.

Skortis Landscaping
Balance Sheet
As of August 31, 2010

	Aug 31, 10
ASSETS	
Current Assets	
Checking/Savings	
1000 · Checking	4,093.52
1010 · Savings	13,000.00
1020 · Petty Cash	185.20
Total Checking/Savings	17,278.72
Accounts Receivable	
1200 · Accounts Receivable	5,546.83
Total Accounts Receivable	5,546.83
Other Current Assets	
1120 · Inventory Asset	
1125 · Plant Inventory	53.97
1130 · Yard Decor Inventory	60.00
Total 1120 · Inventory Asset	113.97
1499 · Undeposited Funds	1,367.23
1500 · Prepaid Insurance	800.00
Total Other Current Assets	2,281.20
Total Current Assets	25,106.75
Fixed Assets	
1800 · Company Truck	
1810 · Accumulated Depreciation	-250.00
1820 · Cost	20,000.00
Total 1800 · Company Truck	19,750.00
Total Fixed Assets	19,750.00
TOTAL ASSETS	44,856.75

Notice that the amount for Total Assets is $44,856.75.

The lower section of the balance sheet represents the right side of the accounting equation and displays all of the liability and equity accounts.

LIABILITIES & EQUITY	
Liabilities	
Current Liabilities	
Accounts Payable	
2000 · Accounts Payable	848.91
Total Accounts Payable	848.91
Credit Cards	
2050 · Poway First National Bank Visa	252.83
Total Credit Cards	252.83
Other Current Liabilities	
2200 · Sales Tax Payable	3.10
Total Other Current Liabilities	3.10
Total Current Liabilities	1,104.84
Long Term Liabilities	
2500 · Truck Loan	17,700.00
Total Long Term Liabilities	17,700.00
Total Liabilities	18,804.84
Equity	
3130 · Owner's Capital	22,000.00
Net Income	4,051.91
Total Equity	26,051.91
TOTAL LIABILITIES & EQUITY	44,856.75

Notice that the amount for Total Liabilities & Equity is also $44,856.75.

The Income Statement

The accounts that you find on the Income Statement (or Profit & Loss report) are income and expense. In the following illustration you can view an Income Statement and the accounts that appear on it.

Skortis Landscaping
Profit & Loss
May 2010

	◇ May 10 ◇
Ordinary Income/Expense	
Income	
4000 · Design Service Income	700.00
4010 · Installation Income	1,365.00
4020 · Maintenance Income	180.00
Total Income	2,245.00
Gross Profit	2,245.00
Expense	
6120 · Bank Service Charges	8.50
6170 · Equipment Rental	300.00
6250 · Postage and Delivery	14.80
6340 · Telephone	164.78
6345 · Freight & Delivery	0.00
6347 · Fuel	33.46
6520 · Job Materials	43.51
6550 · Office Supplies	222.84
6999 · Uncategorized Expenses	213.48
Total Expense	1,001.37
Net Ordinary Income	1,243.63
Net Income	1,243.63

The total of all your income accounts will result in your Gross Profit.

The Total Expense is totaled below the Gross Profit.

The difference between the Gross Profit and Total Expense results in the Net Income (or Net Loss if the expenses are greater than the income).

Debits and Credits: The Double-Entry Accounting System

There is another equation in accounting that is paramount for us to keep in mind: Debits must always equal credits! Most people who do not work in the accounting field are confused about debits and credits, though.

Accounts are often displayed in a "T" format in accounting (which you can see in all of the Behind the Scenes sections of this book). The T accounts allow you to place the name of the account on the top, account debits on the left side, and account credits on the right side. This means that the left side (debits) must always equal the right side (credits) when entering accounting transactions (hence the term "double-entry").

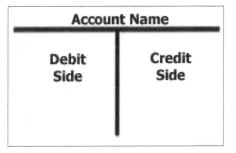

A simple way to view an account is to use the T format.

In order to understand debits and credits a bit better, we will now look at the types of accounts and their normal balances.

Types of Accounts and Normal Balances

We have looked at the two main financial statements and the types of accounts included in each. The balance sheet is composed of asset, liability, and equity accounts. The income statement is composed of income and expense accounts. Before we look deeper into each account type, it is important to understand normal balances.

 TIP! *Take a look at Lesson 5, Creating a Company, to view all of the account sub-types that you can create in QuickBooks.*

About Normal Balances

Each type of account must have a normal balance of either a debit or a credit. The normal balance is the side that will increase the amount of the account. Assets and expenses both have debit normal balances and will increase when debited and decrease when credited. Liabilities, equity, and income all have credit normal balances and will increase when credited and decrease when debited.

The concept of normal balances makes sense if you think of the balance sheet. Assets with a debit normal balance must equal the sum of the liabilities and equity, which both have a credit normal balance. Think of this as the marriage of the accounting equation and the fact that debits must equal credits!

The following table describes the primary account types and their normal balances.

Account Type	Description
Assets	An asset is anything that a company owns or monies that are owed to the company. Examples of assets are checking accounts, accounts receivable, and autos. Assets have a debit normal balance.
Liabilities	A liability is something that a company owes such as an auto loan or a credit card balance. Liabilities have a credit normal balance.
Equity	Equity accounts are both investments into the company (Owner's Equity or Stockholder's Equity) and the net income or loss from the operation of a business (Retained Earnings). Equity accounts have a credit normal balance.
Income	Income accounts reflect the sales and fees earned during an accounting period. Income accounts have a credit normal balance.
Expenses	Expense accounts record the expenditures that a company accrues while conducting business. Expense accounts have a debit normal balance.

The Trial Balance Report

At the end of an accounting cycle a trial balance is prepared that shows all accounts affected during the cycle. The balance of each account is entered in the appropriate column based on its normal balance. The net income or net loss is the difference between income and expenses. If the income is greater than the expenses, an excess credit balance will result and will increase the equity account (a net income). If the expenses are greater than the income, an excess debit balance will result and will decrease the equity account (a net loss).

Look at the following illustration of a trial balance to see how everything we have discussed is pulled together. The difference between the total income ($6,140) and the total expenses ($2,129.57) results in a net income of $ 4,010.43 that will credit (increase) the equity account when the books are closed.

Skortis Landscaping
Trial Balance
As of May 31, 2010

	May 31, 10	
	Debit	Credit
1000 · Checking	5,884.54	
1010 · Savings	13,000.00	
1020 · Petty Cash	185.20	
1200 · Accounts Receivable	3,307.48	
1499 · Undeposited Funds	0.00	
2000 · Accounts Payable		413.96
2050 · Poway First National Bank Visa		452.83
3000 · Opening Bal Equity		15,000.00
3140 · Investments		2,500.00
4000 · Design Service Income		1,540.00
4010 · Installation Income		4,420.00
4020 · Maintenance Income		180.00
6120 · Bank Service Charges	8.50	
6170 · Equipment Rental	300.00	
6250 · Postage and Delivery	14.80	
6290 · Rent	1,000.00	
6340 · Telephone	164.78	
6345 · Freight & Delivery	0.00	
6347 · Fuel	75.59	
6520 · Job Materials	129.58	
6550 · Office Supplies	222.84	
6999 · Uncategorized Expenses	213.48	
TOTAL	**24,506.79**	**24,506.79**

The debits and credits in a Trial Balance must be equal.

Finding Additional Accounting Resources

Want to learn more about what happens to your company's books behind the scenes in Quick-Books? Visit the website for this course at labpub.com/learn/qb10_QC1/ to explore a variety of online learning resources.

Glossary

Accountant's Copy   A special copy of your QuickBooks file that can be created if your accountant needs to make adjustments to your QuickBooks file, but you do not want to lose access to it while it is being adjusted

Accrual Basis   In the accrual basis of accounting, income is recorded when the sale is made and expenses recorded when accrued; often used by firms or businesses with large inventories

Activities   Affect what is happening behind the scenes; can be easily input into forms such as invoices or bills

Administrator   QuickBooks user who controls the access of all users of a QuickBooks file; administrator also controls all company preferences in the Edit Preferences window

Assets   Anything owned by a company or that is owed to a company; items such as a checking account, a building, a prepaid insurance account, or accounts receivable

Audit Trail   Allows you to track every entry, modification, or deletion to transactions in your file; accessed through the Accounting category in the Report Center or the Report option on the menu bar

Backup   The process of creating a condensed copy of your QuickBooks file to ensure you don't lose your data or to allow yourself or another person the ability to view your company file on another computer

Balance Sheet Accounts   The asset, liability, and equity accounts, such as bank, credit card, current liabilities (sales tax payable and payroll liabilities), accounts receivable, accounts payable, and retained earnings

Behind the Scenes   The accounting that QuickBooks performs for you when you enter transactions

Browser   A software application used to locate and display web pages, such as Netscape Navigator and Microsoft Internet Explorer

Cash Basis   In the cash basis of accounting, income is recorded when cash is received and expenses recorded when cash is paid; commonly used by small businesses and professionals

Centers   QuickBooks has four centers: Customer, Employee, Report, and Vendor; centers allow you to view the Customer & Job, Employee, and Vendor lists, access QuickBooks reports, and view snapshots of information (of an individual customer, vendor, or employee)

Classes   Classes are used to rate; not tied to any particular customer, vendor, or item; used to track only one particular aspect of your business, such as location or individual programs

Closing the Books   During this process at the end of your fiscal year, QuickBooks transfers the net income or net loss to Retained Earnings, restricts access to transactions prior to the closing date (unless you know the password) and allows you to clean up your company data; you are not required to "close the books" in QuickBooks

Company Setup   Takes you through the steps necessary to set up a new company in QuickBooks

Customer & Job List   A list in QuickBooks that stores all information related to your customers and the jobs associated with them

Customer & Vendor Profile Lists   Lists QuickBooks provides to track customer and vendor information

Depreciation   Provides a business with a way to match income to expenses; a fixed asset is used to produce income over a period of time, and depreciation allows you to record the appropriate expense for the same period; many small businesses record depreciation transactions just once a year, but they can be entered monthly or quarterly if the business produces financial statements for those periods

Draw An owner's withdrawal of funds from the company

EasyStep Interview This method of company creation takes you through a series of questions; your answer to each question determines how your company is set up

Edition Intuit creates a multitude of editions of QuickBooks to choose from: QuickBooks Basic, QuickBooks Pro, and QuickBooks Premier

Electronic Payments Some companies receive payments from customers electronically; they can be handled by using a new payment type called Electronic Payment

Employee List A list in QuickBooks that helps you to keep track of your employee data; can be used as a source of information to run payroll in QuickBooks; accessed through the Employee Center

Equity Accounts Reflect the owner's investment in the company and have a credit normal balance; in a Sole Proprietorship, equity is what the owner has invested in the company and in a corporation, the equity is what the shareholders have invested in the company

Field A box into which data is entered

File Storage Location Location in which you store file for this course (USB flash drive, the My Documents folder, or to a network drive at a school or company)

Filtering Filtering allows you to include only the essential data in your report; choose to filter out many types of data such as accounts, dollar amounts, and types of customers; allows you to closely examine and report on a specific group of data

Fixed Asset An asset you don't plan to use up or turn into cash within the next year; businesses use fixed assets in a productive capacity to promote the main operations of the company; are depreciable, which means that you don't expense the assets when you purchase them, but rather over the useful life of the asset

Fixed Asset Account Type of account that tracks the activities associated with a fixed asset

Fonts QuickBooks displays its preset reports in a default font; you can make many changes as to the characteristics of the font in your report, such as the font name, style, color, and size

Formatting Formatting deals with the appearance of the report; it has nothing to do with the data contained within it

Graphs Graphs in QuickBooks allow you to display your information in a more illustrative way

Header and Footer Default headers and footers appear on all preset QuickBooks reports; change the information included along with how it is formatted on the Header and Footer tabs of the Additional Customization window

Homepage A web page that serves as an index or table of contents to other documents stored on the site; the main page for a large website; the web page that comes up by default when you open your browser

Hypertext Markup Language (HTML) A text-based language that any computer can read; used to organize pages with devices such as headings, paragraphs, lists, etc.

Internet A collection of computers all over the world that send, receive, and store information; access is gained through an Internet Service Provider (ISP); the web is just a portion of the Internet

Investment Occurs when an owner deposits funds into the company

Joint Photographic Experts Group (JPG) Committee that designed the graphics format; JPG images support 16 million colors and are best suited for photographs and complex graphics

Layout Designer The Layout Designer window provides rulers to line up objects, and toolbar buttons to help manipulate your template objects

Link Also called hyperlink; provides navigation through a website; displayed on the QuickBooks Home page to provide navigation throughout the QuickBooks program

List (Database)   Allows you to store information about customers, vendors, employees, and other data important to your business

Logo   QuickBooks allows you to personalize your templates by including your company logo

Long Term Liabilities Account   A QuickBooks account that tracks a liability (loan) you do not plan to pay off within the next year

On the Fly   When you type a new entry into a field that draws from a list, QuickBooks gives you the opportunity to add the record to the list "on the fly" as you create the transaction

Other Current Assets Account   An account that tracks the transactions related to an asset that you plan to either use up or convert to cash within one year

Passing an Expense On to Customers   The process of identifying an expense in a transaction for which you plan to charge a customer and invoicing the customer for the expense

Payroll Liabilities   The account in which you hold payroll taxes and other deductions until you are required to pay them

Payroll Options   Intuit provides five options to run your payroll: Manual, Standard, Enhanced Plus, Assisted, and Complete; to compare these options, visit the book's website at labpub.com/learn/qb9/

Petty Cash   Cash kept by businesses for small expenditures; in QuickBooks, Petty Cash is set up as a bank account in the Chart of Accounts

Preferences   The way you interact with Quick-Books is controlled by the preferences you select; the Preferences window has 19 categories; company preferences are controlled by the administrator and determine how the entire company interacts with QuickBooks; personal preferences are controlled by individual users and dictate interactions between QuickBooks and only that one user

Profit and Loss (P&L) Report   A financial report that can be found in the Company & Financial category of the Report Finder window; P&L reports reflect all transactions that have affected income and expense accounts within a specified time period

Quick Reference Tables   Tables that summarize the tasks you have just learned. Use them as guidelines when you begin work on your own QuickBooks company file.

Quick Report   A report that shows all the transactions recorded in QuickBooks for a particular list record, which can be run from the various list windows

QuickBooks Shipping Manager   Allows you to use your FedEx or UPS account to ship directly from QuickBooks; allows you to create a shipment and shipping label (with all of the information pre-filled) right from the Create Invoices and Enter Sales Receipts windows; can be used to track your shipments

QuickZoom   A QuickBooks report and graph feature that allows you to zoom through underlying sub-reports until you reach the form where the data were originally entered; this can be extremely useful if you have questions about where a figure in a report or graph comes from

Reconciliation   The process of matching your QuickBooks accounts to the bank and credit card statements you receive. It is important to make sure that your account records in QuickBooks match those of the bank or credit card company

Report   A way to display your company information in various ways such as printed, onscreen, or as a PDF file

Resize   To change the height or width of an image, window, or object

Restoring   The process of decompressing a Quick-Books backup or portable company file; when you restore a file in the same location with the same name as another file, it will replace that file

Sales Orders Allows you to manage customer orders of both products and services; available in the Premier and Enterprise editions

Skip Interview In this method of company creation, QuickBooks asks you for your basic company information, and it will be up to you to set up certain items such as payroll and inventory later

Starter Chart of Accounts During the setup process, QuickBooks asks you to choose the business type that your company most closely resembles; QuickBooks uses your choice to create a Chart of Accounts close to what you need (it will take you less time to edit it to fit your unique business than to start from scratch); you cannot change the business type option later

Subaccounts Help you keep precise records; to track expenses more closely, you may want to have separate accounts for your office phone, office fax, cellular phone, etc.; subaccounts are a great way to track these separate expenses while keeping the number of expense accounts down

Template A specific form format (with no data) on which you can base all of your future forms; QuickBooks provides several templates, but you can also create custom templates

Uniform Resource Locator (URL) A web address used to identify a unique page on the Internet

Users You can set up an unlimited number of users for your QuickBooks company and assign a password for each person; users can only change their own personal preferences (the administrator controls the access each user has to the QuickBooks file)

Vendor Anyone (except employees) to whom you pay money; could be the electric company, the organization to which you pay taxes, a merchandise supplier, or subcontractors you pay to do work for your customers

Vendor List A list in QuickBooks that stores all information related to your vendors

Version Intuit creates a new version of QuickBooks each year (such as QuickBooks 2006, 2007, or 2008) and each new version provides additional features that are new for that year

Website Refers to a collection of related web pages and their supporting files and folders.

World Wide Web (WWW) Also called the web; organized system of Internet servers that support HTML documents; the fun part of the Internet

Year-to-Date Amounts If you begin to use the QuickBooks payroll feature for existing employees who have received at least one paycheck from you (and it is not the first day of January), you must enter year-to-date amounts for them to ensure that QuickBooks calculates taxes with thresholds properly and you will be able to print accurate W-2s at the end of the year

Index